TABLE OF CO

FORWA
2

CHAPTER 1: 1980'S VS 2000'S
4

CHAPTER 2: OUT DAMN SPOT!
13

CHAPTER 3: CAN YOU MICROWAVE A TURKEY?
25

CHAPTER 4: DOMESTIC TRANQUILITY
43

CHAPTER 5: THE DOCTOR IS IN
51

CHAPTER 6: DID HE/SHE/THEY REALLY JUST TEXT THAT?
68

CHAPTER 7: ADULTING IS HARD
88

CHAPTER 8: NEW SIM CARD, SAME TEXTS
96

CHAPTER 9: LIFE'S NOT FAIR
104

CHAPTER 10: YES, THERE ARE CLASSES HERE TOO
113

CHAPTER 11: HELP!!!! IT'S URGENT!
122

CHAPTER 12: JUST WANTED TO SAY...
131

ACKNOWLEDGMENTS
143

The inspiration for this book began when my daughter went to college. My husband flew to California with her, picked up the online orders from Bed, Bath and Beyond, the Container Store and Staples and delivered them to the dorm while she went off on a university sponsored pre-orientation trip. I arrived a few days later ready to meet her post-trip and "help" her move into the dorm. By "help", I mean cover the mattress with the bed bug protector, layer a 2-inch foam pad on top of that, followed by a fitted sheet, flat sheet and duvet coordinated to match her roommate's. I also "helped" raise the bed to fit the multiple under bed storage shelves, expanded the closet space with a double hung rod and affixed the carefully chosen photo collage of family and friends onto the wall.

The entire move-in experience was a dramatic departure from my freshman college arrival in the 80's. I moved into my dorm with a Marimekko comforter, adorned with red, blue, and yellow tulips from my bedroom at home, and a bright yellow milk crate I had liberated from my local A&P Grocery Store – it was the perfect size for holding record albums. Shortly after I made my bed, my mom gave me a hug goodbye and left California for her flight back to Chicago. She did not stay to decorate my room. She did not stay to meet my roommate. She returned to my dad and their empty nest and reminded me to "call home on Sunday after 5."

Communication between parents and children changed pretty radically since the 80's. I received my first message from my daughter when she was on the bus ride home from the pre-orientation. It was not a Sunday. It was not after 5. And, she did not call. She texted:

Little did I know, that whether I was on campus or thousands of miles away, texting was about to become our primary mode of communication.

It hit me, as I was navigating this new terrain, that Sunday after 5 was about as quaint a custom as families sitting down to watch sit-coms together after dinner. Why wait to call on Sunday if the concept of "when the rates go down" no longer applies? I grew up a part of the "Kick the Can" generation; we played outside until dark or dinner, whichever came first. We rode our bicycles everywhere. When our parents went out, they might have given the babysitter an emergency phone number – whose, I can't imagine, since my grandparents, who lived 20 miles away were likely out as well-- but I highly doubt it was ever used.

Once college arrived, the children my husband and I had raised – with independence, manners, and understanding the importance of hand-written thank-you notes – seemed remotely at sea. The channels of communication over the next four years, I understood at once, were going be open 24/7. There'd be no need for a weekly review. Instead, there'd be hourly updates. Sometimes, minute-by-minute updates. It was only after I started sharing some of these texts with my friends that I learned I was not alone. We were all besieged with hilarious texts.

This collection contains authentic messages from college students across the country, mostly strangers, some my own children. It is not a commentary on parenting college students, rather a humorous take on parent/child exchanges in the cell phone age. It is offered with gratitude for the privilege of being able to send a child to college and for the fact that they choose to text us rather than ask Siri.

All proceeds from the sale of this book will be donated to organizations offering opportunities for low-income students to attend college.

*Names have been removed to protect privacy.

*Typos remain to preserve authenticity.

CHAPTER 1

1980's vs 2000's

Simply said, there was no "on-line". You waited in-line to use the pay phones in the dormitory hall. You waited in line, a rather long one, to register for classes and pay for your books. And, while you were waiting, you did not have a cell phone to text your parents.

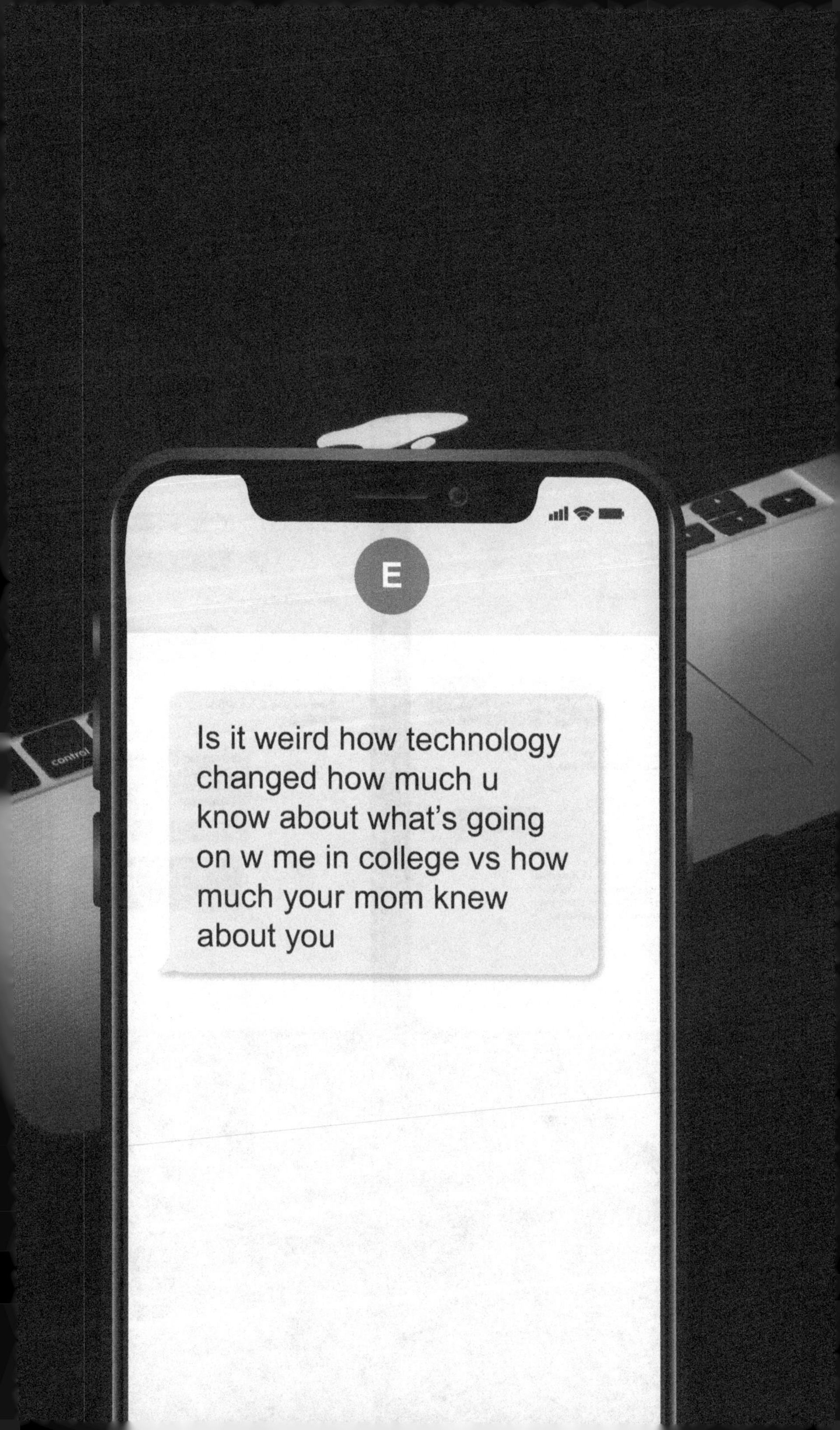

E

Is it weird how technology changed how much u know about what's going on w me in college vs how much your mom knew about you

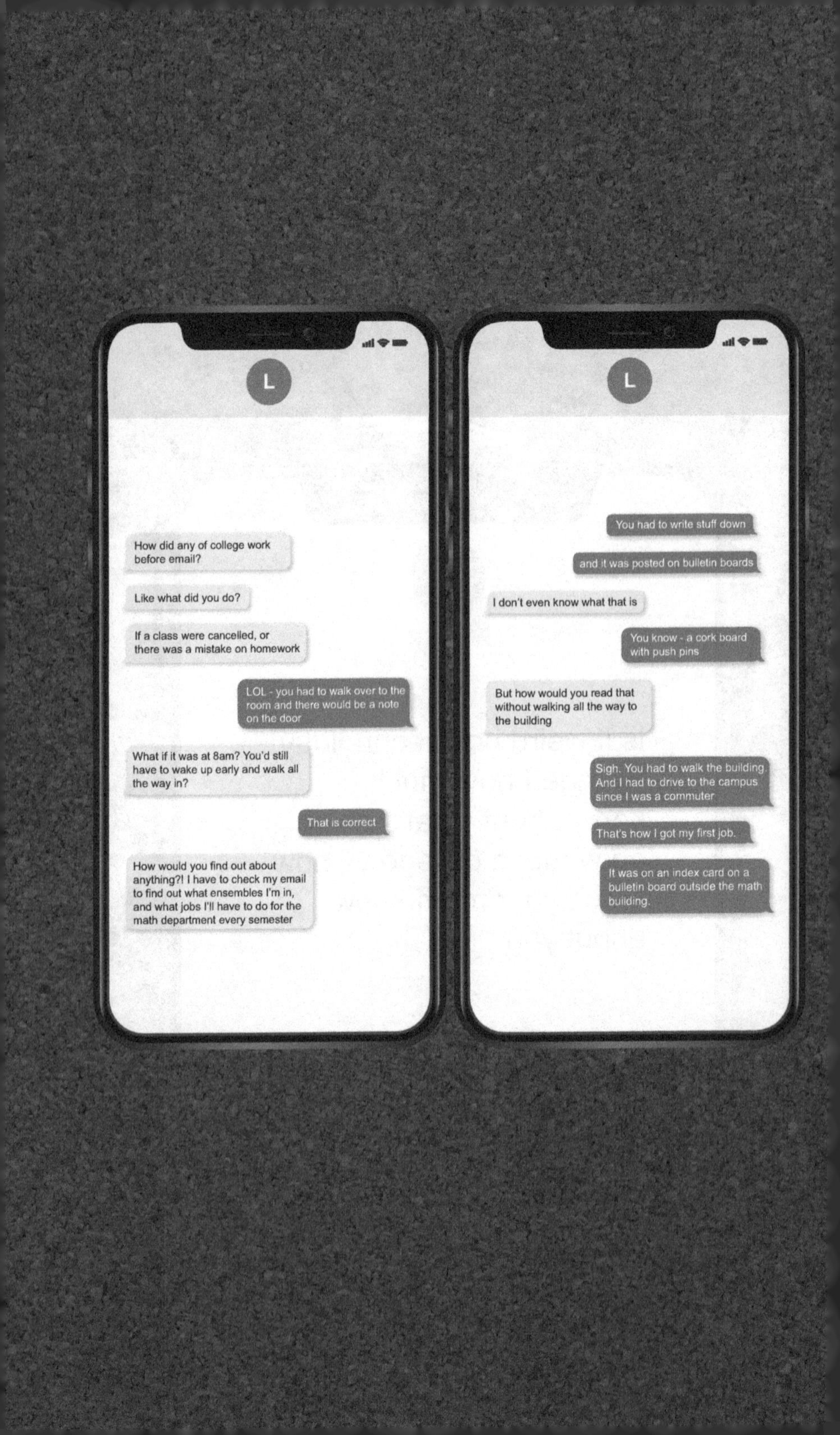

L

How did any of college work before email?

Like what did you do?

If a class were cancelled, or there was a mistake on homework

LOL - you had to walk over to the room and there would be a note on the door

What if it was at 8am? You'd still have to wake up early and walk all the way in?

That is correct

How would you find out about anything?! I have to check my email to find out what ensembles I'm in, and what jobs I'll have to do for the math department every semester

L

You had to write stuff down

and it was posted on bulletin boards

I don't even know what that is

You know - a cork board with push pins

But how would you read that without walking all the way to the building

Sigh. You had to walk the building. And I had to drive to the campus since I was a commuter

That's how I got my first job.

It was on an index card on a bulletin board outside the math building.

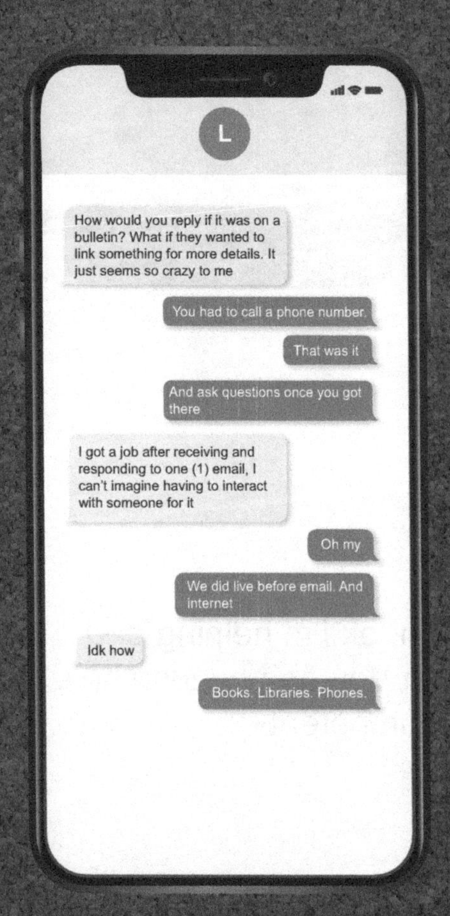
L
How would you reply if it was on a bulletin? What if they wanted to link something for more details. It just seems so crazy to me
You had to call a phone number.
That was it
And ask questions once you got there
I got a job after receiving and responding to one (1) email, I can't imagine having to interact with someone for it
Oh my
We did live before email. And internet
Idk how
Books. Libraries. Phones.

P

Ugh, ok I'm helping dad with Venmo because he's incompetent

R

I acutally do need $12 for WiFi I haven't paid yet.

to Joe

Pleas

What?

I owe joe like $12 for WiFi

Done. Please don't ask for any more money for at least 2 hours

ok

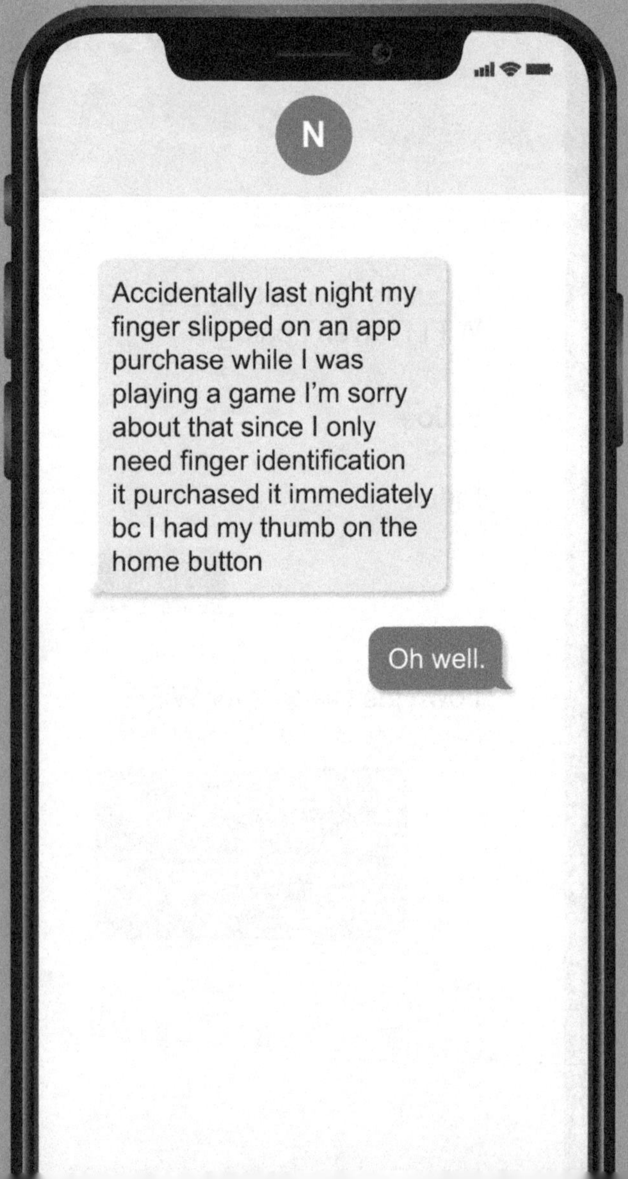

N

Accidentally last night my finger slipped on an app purchase while I was playing a game I'm sorry about that since I only need finger identification it purchased it immediately bc I had my thumb on the home button

Oh well.

Y

Can you talk right now?

Like on the phone?

Yea

Yea in a minute

I'll call you

ok

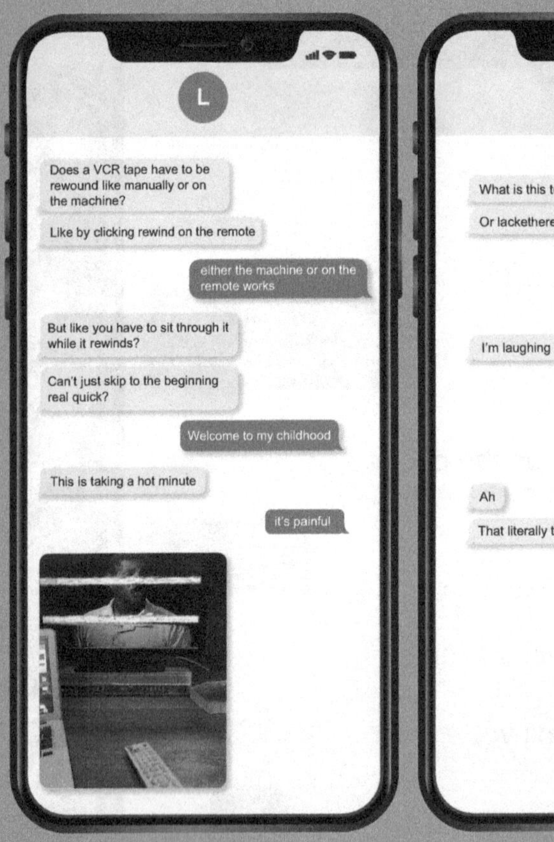
L
Does a VCR tape have to be rewound like manually or on the machine?
Like by clicking rewind on the remote
either the machine or on the remote works
But like you have to sit through it while it rewinds?
Can't just skip to the beginning real quick?
Welcome to my childhood
This is taking a hot minute
it's painful

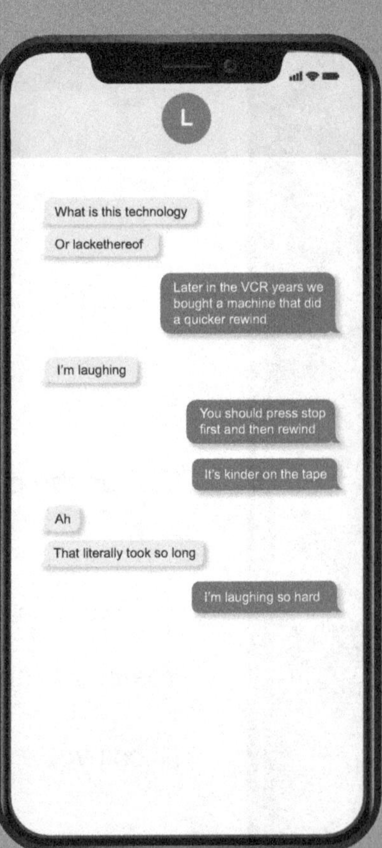
L
What is this technology
Or lackethereof
Later in the VCR years we bought a machine that did a quicker rewind
I'm laughing
You should press stop first and then rewind
It's kinder on the tape
Ah
That literally took so long
I'm laughing so hard

CHAPTER 2

Out damn spot!

It does not matter if you taught your child how to do laundry before they left for school. It does not matter if they have done laundry at home for years.

School is different. The machines are different. And, they are different every year, in each new dorm or apartment.

And what about stains and blood? That was not covered in laundry 101.

B

here's the machine. what do I do

i don't have any detergent or tide pods

U have ALL pods. Not Tide. Same thing. Different brand. And that's ok 👍
Oh and I put them in the side pocket of ur laundry bag so u would have them with you ☺

clothes are in. two pods are in WITH the clothes

guess I'll start it

how long should it take to run

Varies. just under an hour. Check back in 45 minutes

it said 34 minutes

there ya go

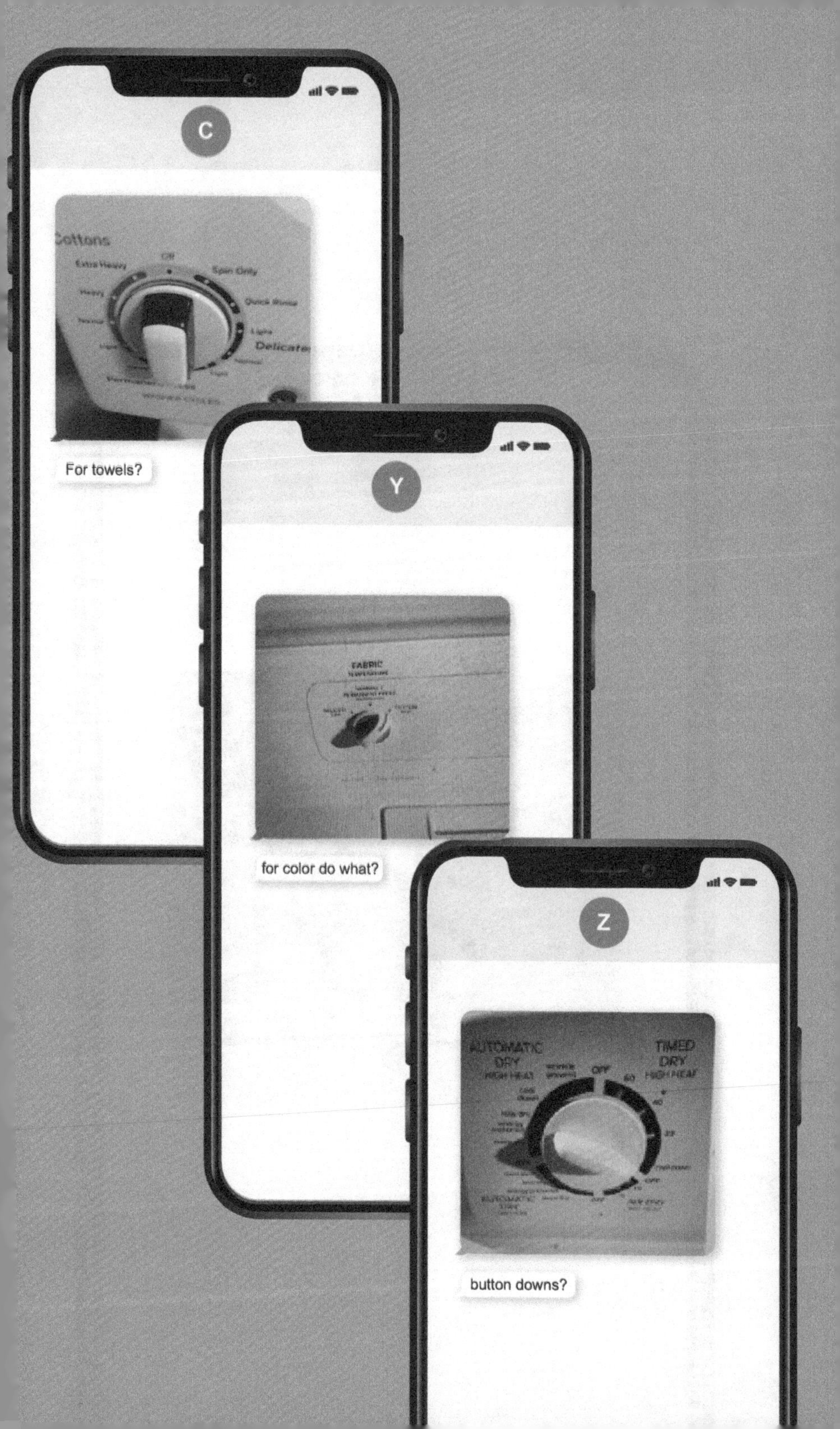
C
Cottons
Extra Heavy
Off
Spin Only
Quick Rinse
Delicates
For towels?
Y
FABRIC
for color do what?
Z
AUTOMATIC
DRY
HIGH HEAT
OFF
60
TIMED
DRY
button downs?

T

which one

P

What happens when overload laundry?!

probably won't get as clean

why

Just wondered if my laundry was gonna explode

L

Got beer spilled all over jean jacket is that washable?

yes

Just regularly?

yes

L

I’m freaking out

It’s staining

It’s ruined

I’m so upset mom this is the end

Helllllllll

P

R

hi

What you doing?

laundry

Lol bed sheets?

no clothes

am i supposed to
wash my sheets?

You should wash sheets
and pillow cases since
you have been sick!

oh true

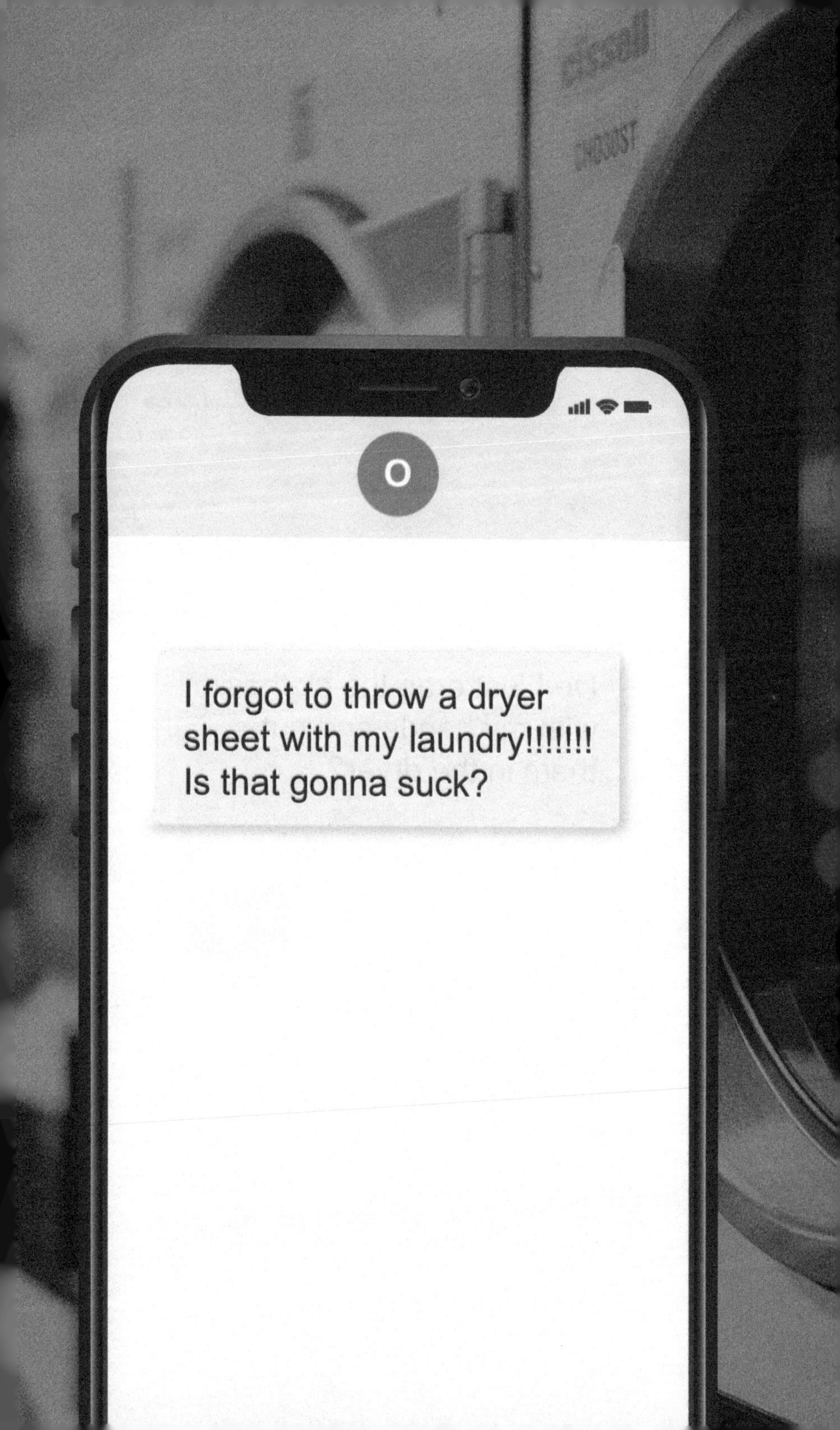

O

I forgot to throw a dryer sheet with my laundry!!!!!!!
Is that gonna suck?

B

Do I just grab the clothes with my hands and put them in the dryer?

yes

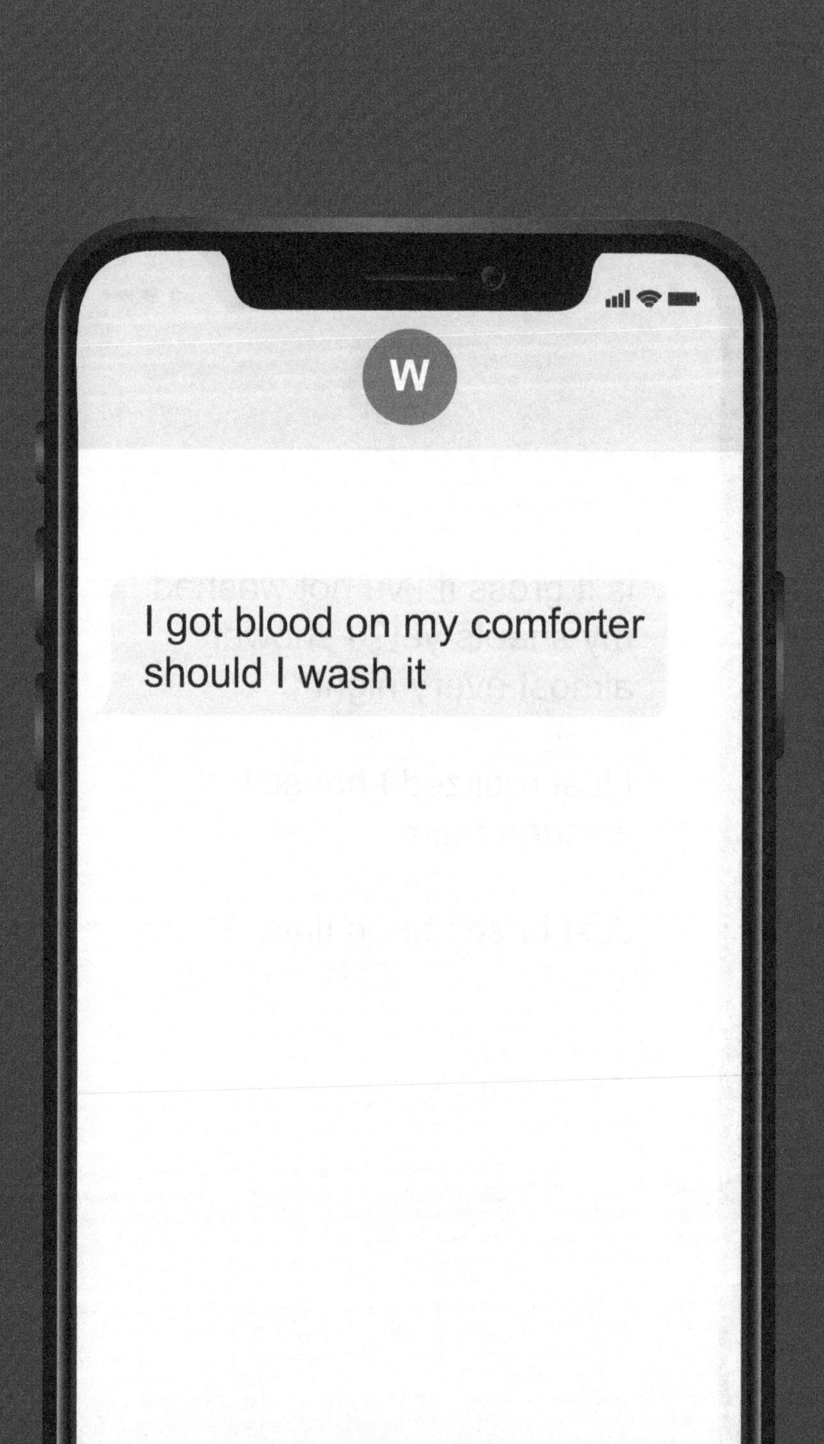
W
I got blood on my comforter should I wash it

is it gross if I’ve not washed my sheets yet? I shower almost every night

I just realized I haven’t washed them

Just hasn’t been time

Can you microwave a turkey?

Teaching your children some basic cooking skills and sending them off to college with a set of go-to recipes will save them time and money; becoming an on-call Julia Child will not serve either of you well.

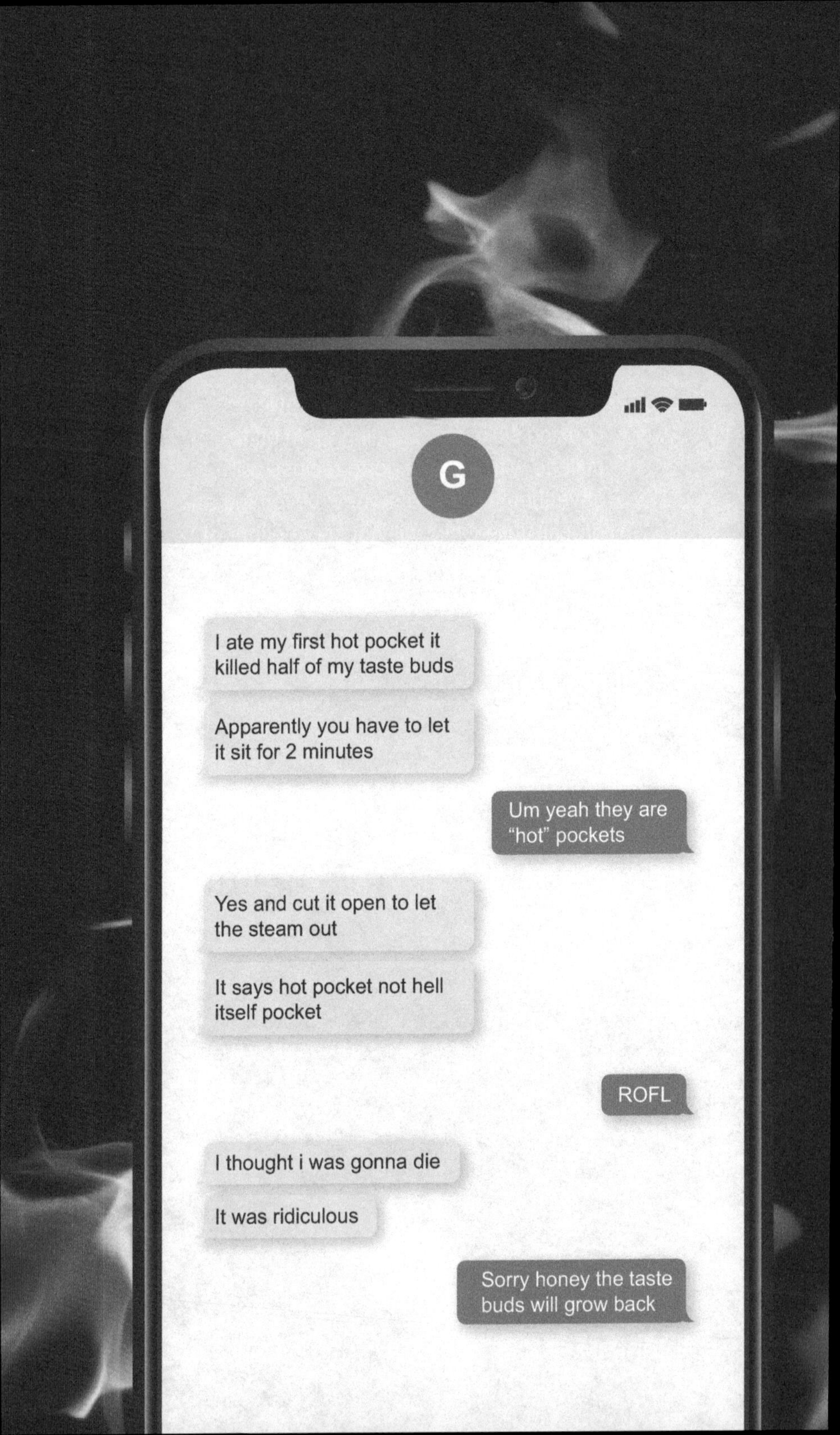

G

I ate my first hot pocket it killed half of my taste buds

Apparently you have to let it sit for 2 minutes

Um yeah they are "hot" pockets

Yes and cut it open to let the steam out

It says hot pocket not hell itself pocket

ROFL

I thought i was gonna die

It was ridiculous

Sorry honey the taste buds will grow back

K
I made a sandwich and I realized I forgot the chicken lol
Wait you didn't put the chicken in the sandwich?
No
I forgot
So you just have bread and tomato, spinach and mayo?
And mustard and salt and pepper
It's not too bad tbh

D
Can you get me a big Tupperware container for my birthday I want to cook big meals in the morning so I'll have food all day
Love that you are cooking!

C

Would I like scallops

If they are in olive oil
and garlic, yes!

Not risking it.

A
I cannot wait for actual food
literally 75% reason I'm coming home

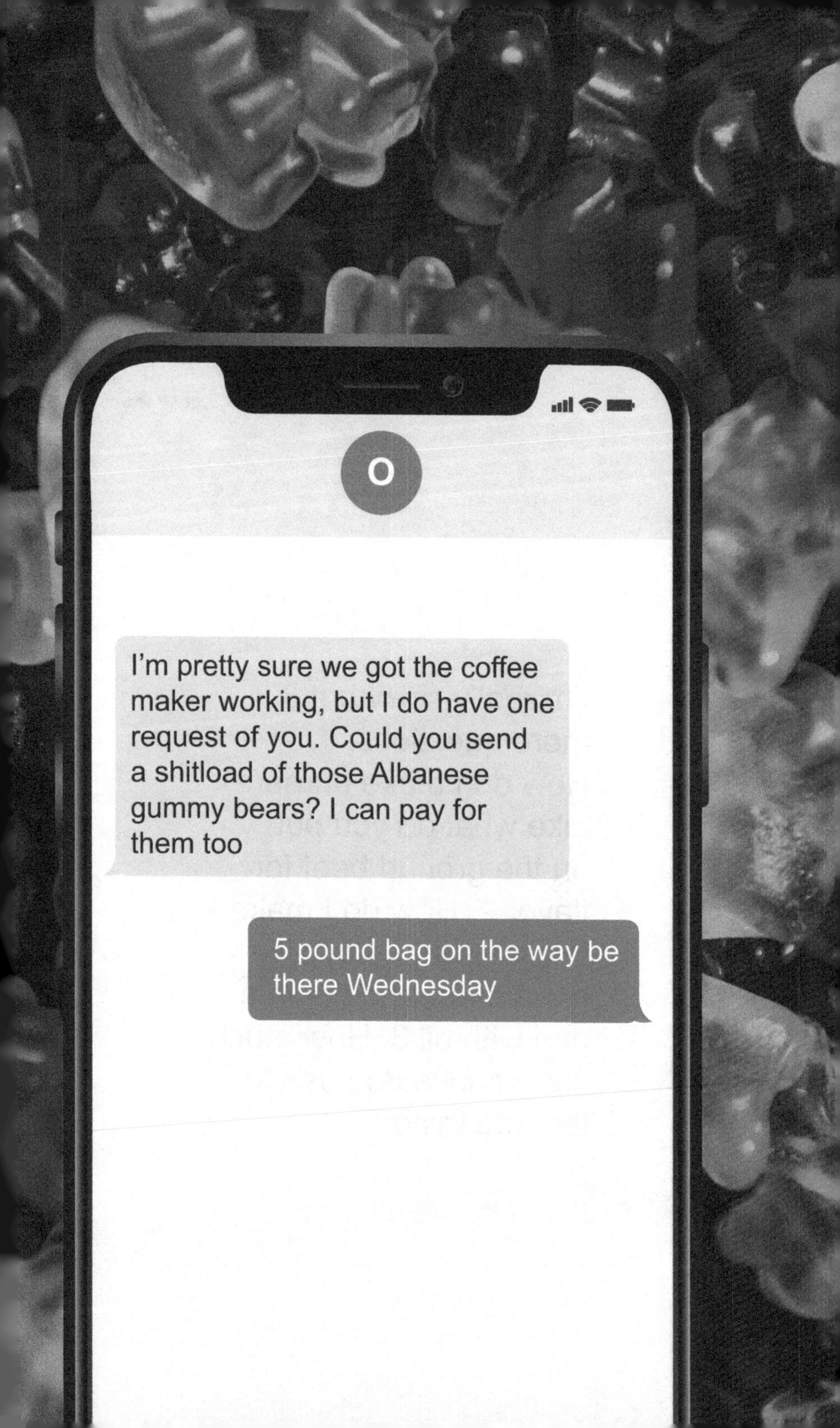
O
I'm pretty sure we got the coffee maker working, but I do have one request of you. Could you send a shitload of those Albanese gummy bears? I can pay for them too
5 pound bag on the way be there Wednesday

D

I'm really sorry but 3 more questions: 1. How do I make burgers? Like what do you put on the ground beef for flavor 2. How do I make Brussels in the over to roast them and not in a pan with oil 3. How much curry sauce do I use for the tofu thing

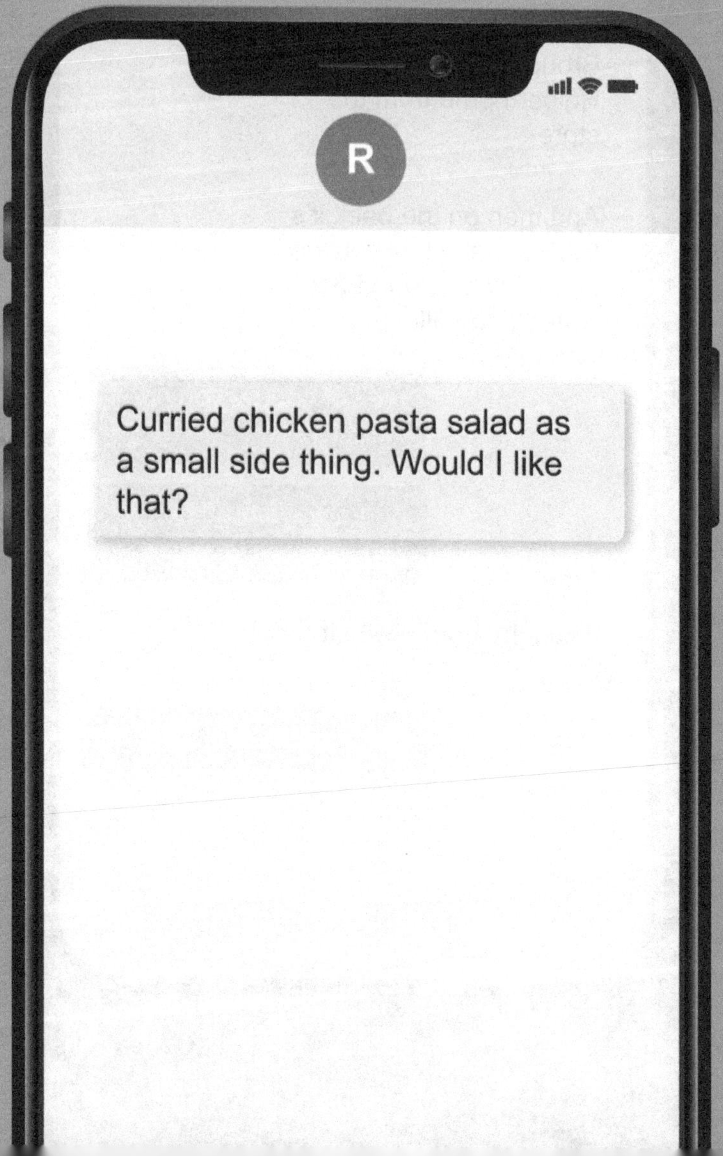

R

Curried chicken pasta salad as a small side thing. Would I like that?

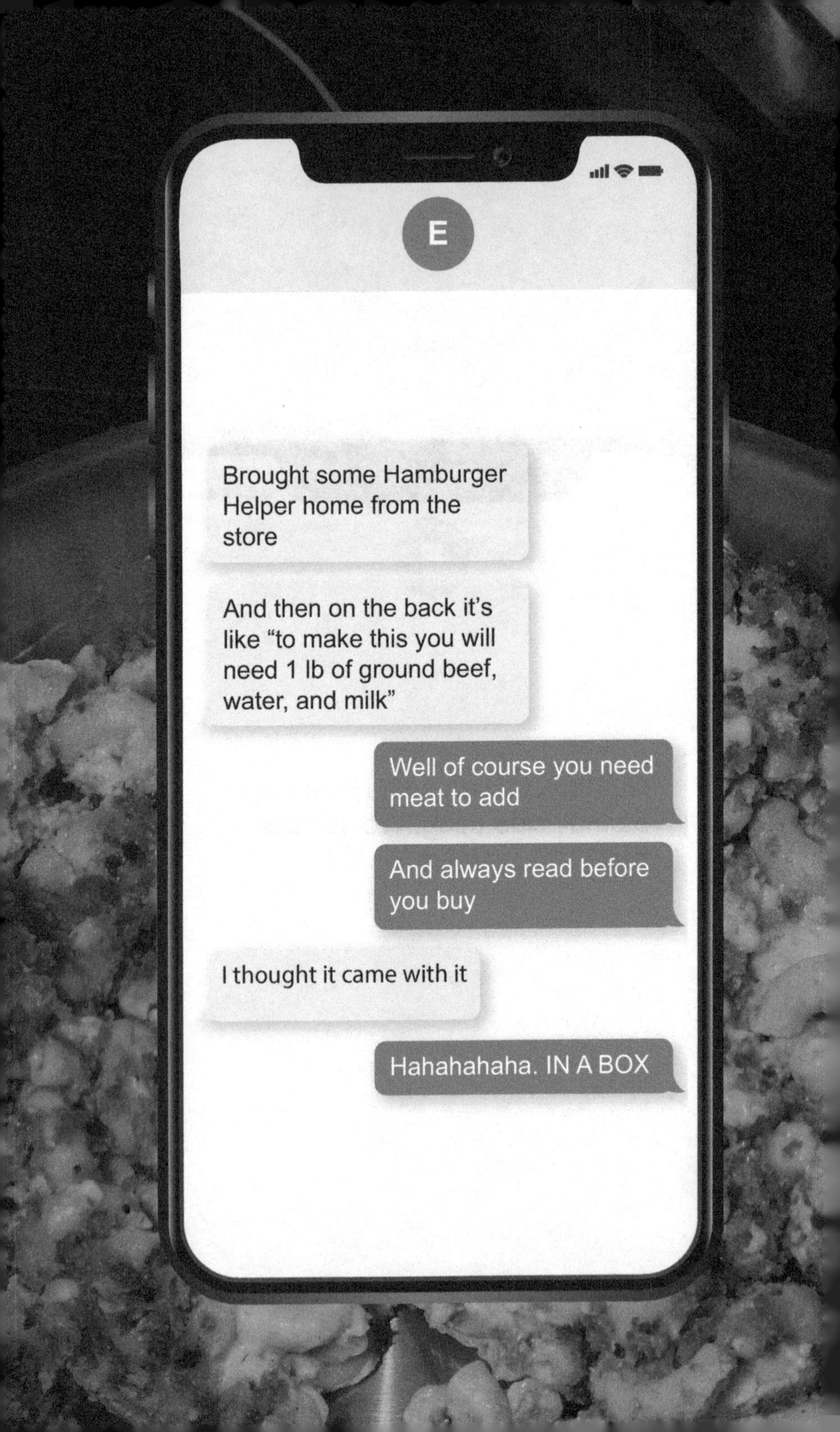

E

Brought some Hamburger Helper home from the store

And then on the back it's like "to make this you will need 1 lb of ground beef, water, and milk"

Well of course you need meat to add

And always read before you buy

I thought it came with it

Hahahahaha. IN A BOX

N

I got some Hamburger Helper too

You always did like that stuff

I saw it and I got 2 of the beef macaroni ones

You did get the ground beef too, right?

No it comes in the box

right?

well shit

V
I bought broccoli and I was cuting it and I found a caterpillar is it safe to eat the broccoli
Are you cooking it or eating raw?

R

How long to microwave spinach and potatoes?

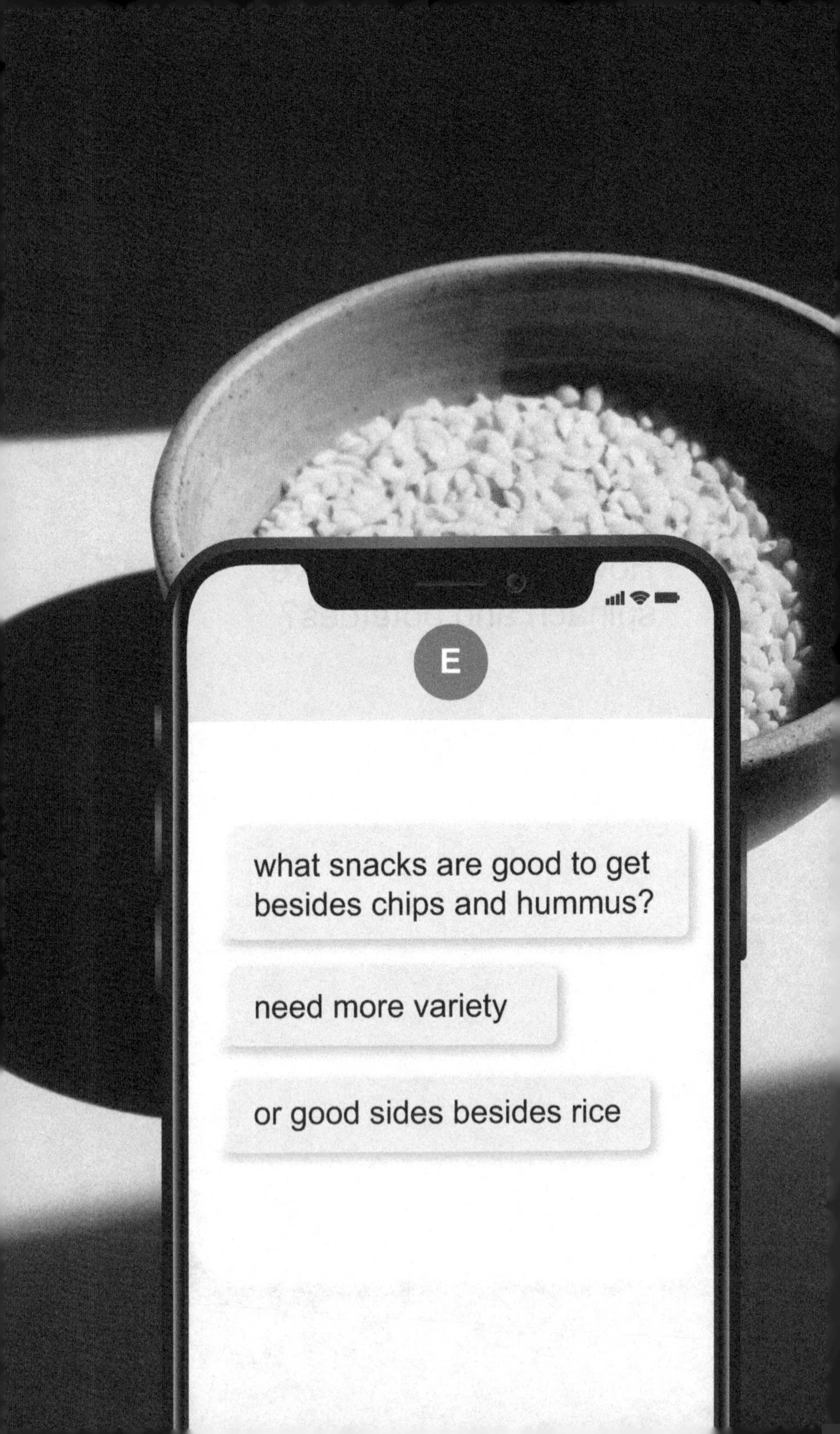
E
what snacks are good to get besides chips and hummus?
need more variety
or good sides besides rice

R
Mom, do I eat this cold

W

Do you use butter when making Annies mac and cheese? Box says options so what do you normally do?

L
so I tried to bake.
I set the fire alarm off twice

W
Just filled up water in a really old building and it's like white should I not drink

Domestic tranquility

Roommate - defined as a person sharing a room, suite, apartment or house with another - can make or break a college experience. Between late night parties or early morning alarms, uninvited guests and varying definitions of clean, even the seemingly perfect matches don't always flourish.

Q

Something's wrong with my toilet etf is the nast shit

my dear, that is, your mother cleaned your toilet for 18 years! Now you need to clean it

I'm not touching that. Toilets are disgusting

B

U were right
Wiping off counters
is part of doing dishes

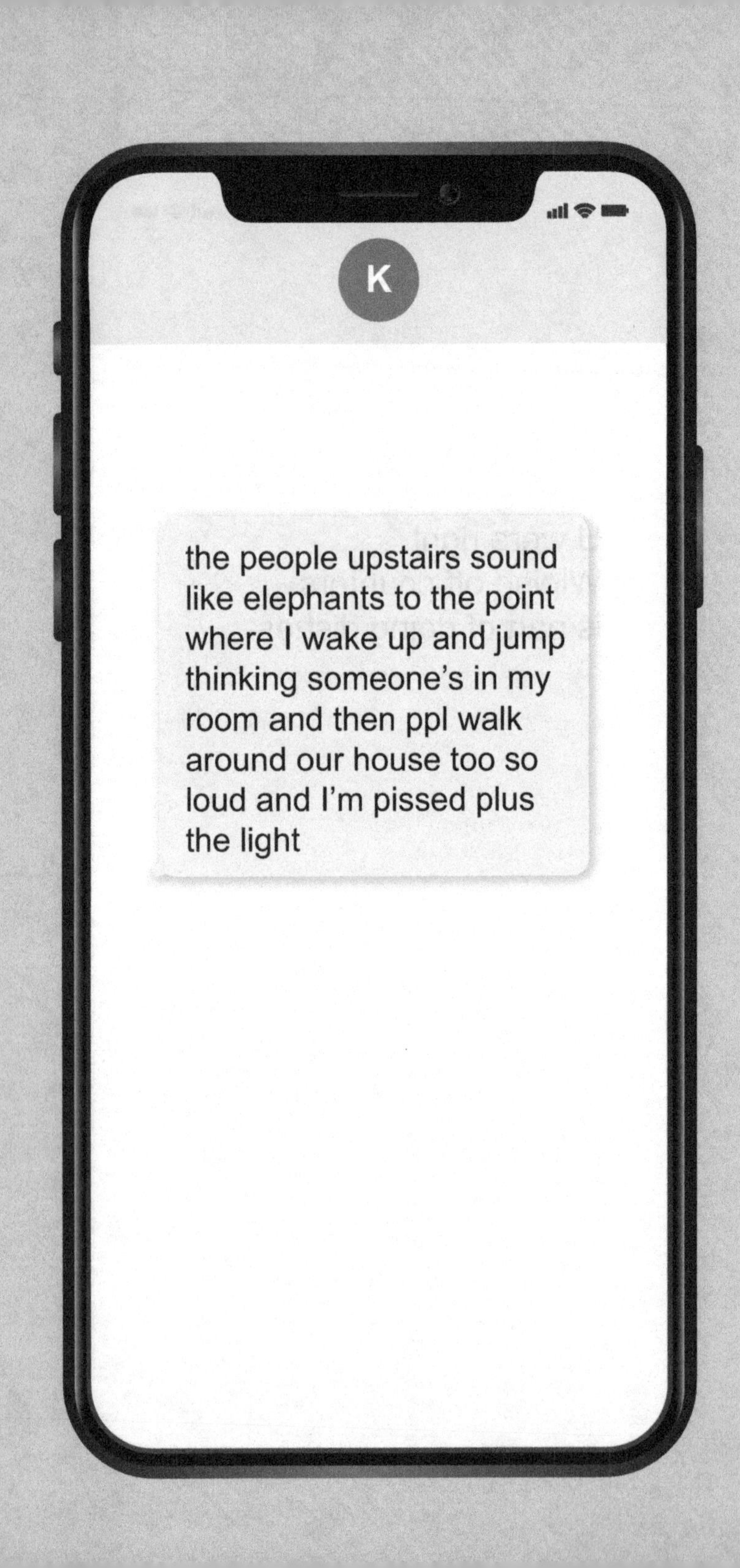
K
the people upstairs sound like elephants to the point where I wake up and jump thinking someone's in my room and then ppl walk around our house too so loud and I'm pissed plus the light

P

I hate life right now because I just wanna sleep but this god dam light if so fucking bright

It should NOT be this bright at 2am meanwhile I still need sleep and I fell asleep at 12:35 and the light woke me up at 1:25

Am I gonna die?

Fuck it apparently I don't need sleep

A

Hi sorry so I just got back and the toilet overflowed onto the bathroom. I put in a work request but the floor is disgusting and XXXXXX went to yoga after it happened so I called a cleaning service and they're coming rn

OMG WTF

what did she do

Is it spilling out of the bathroom?????

Would like to get a mini fridge so I can keep some of my food to myself

People are eating my deli meat from whole foods

I have to go buy one today

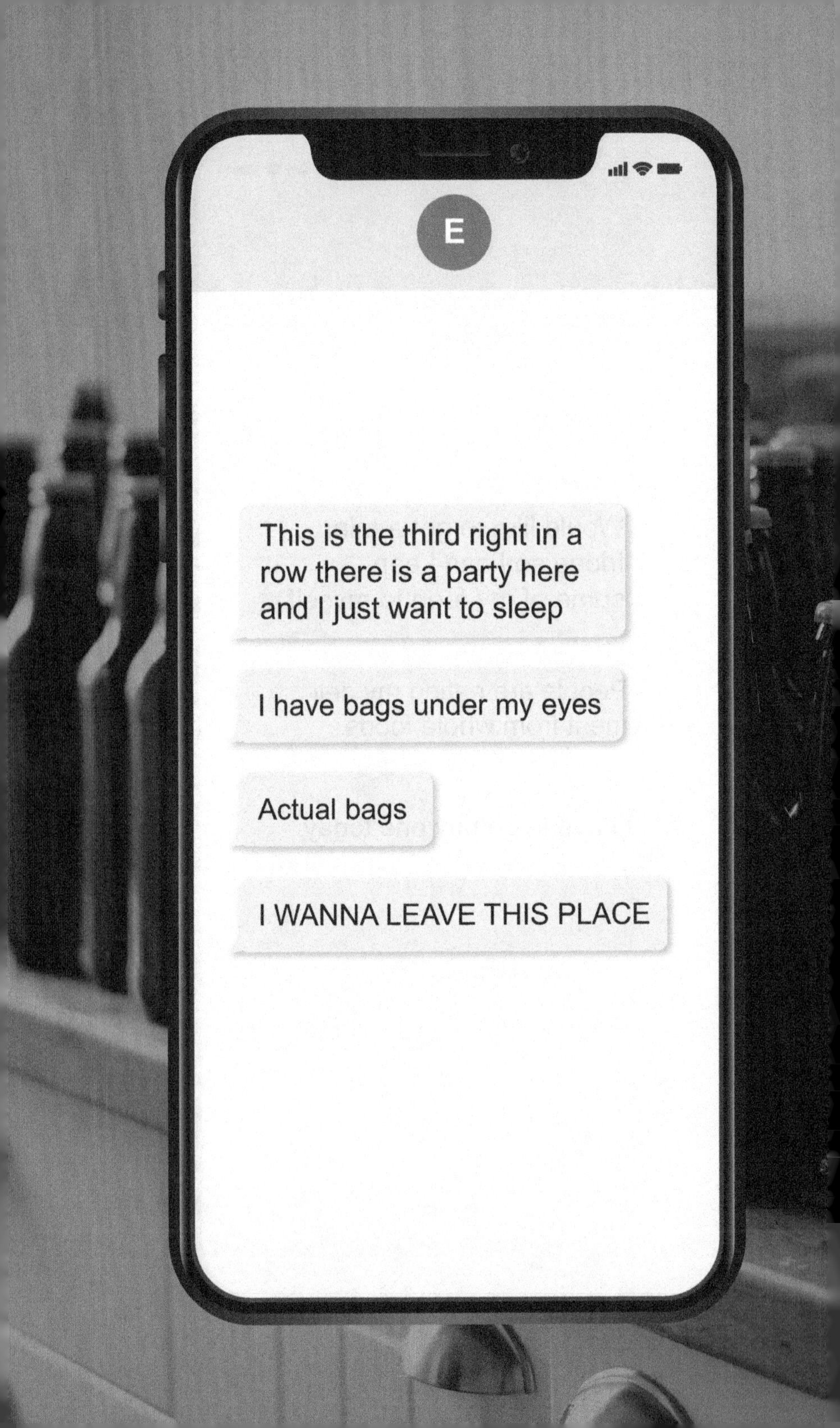
E
This is the third right in a row there is a party here and I just want to sleep
I have bags under my eyes
Actual bags
I WANNA LEAVE THIS PLACE

CHAPTER 5

The doctor is in

Most parents are not doctors. We do not even play them on TV. We are neither qualified to diagnose nor to treat medical conditions.

Nevertheless, the health texts abound. Sometimes with photographic evidence. Often, after having spent countless hours on Web MD.

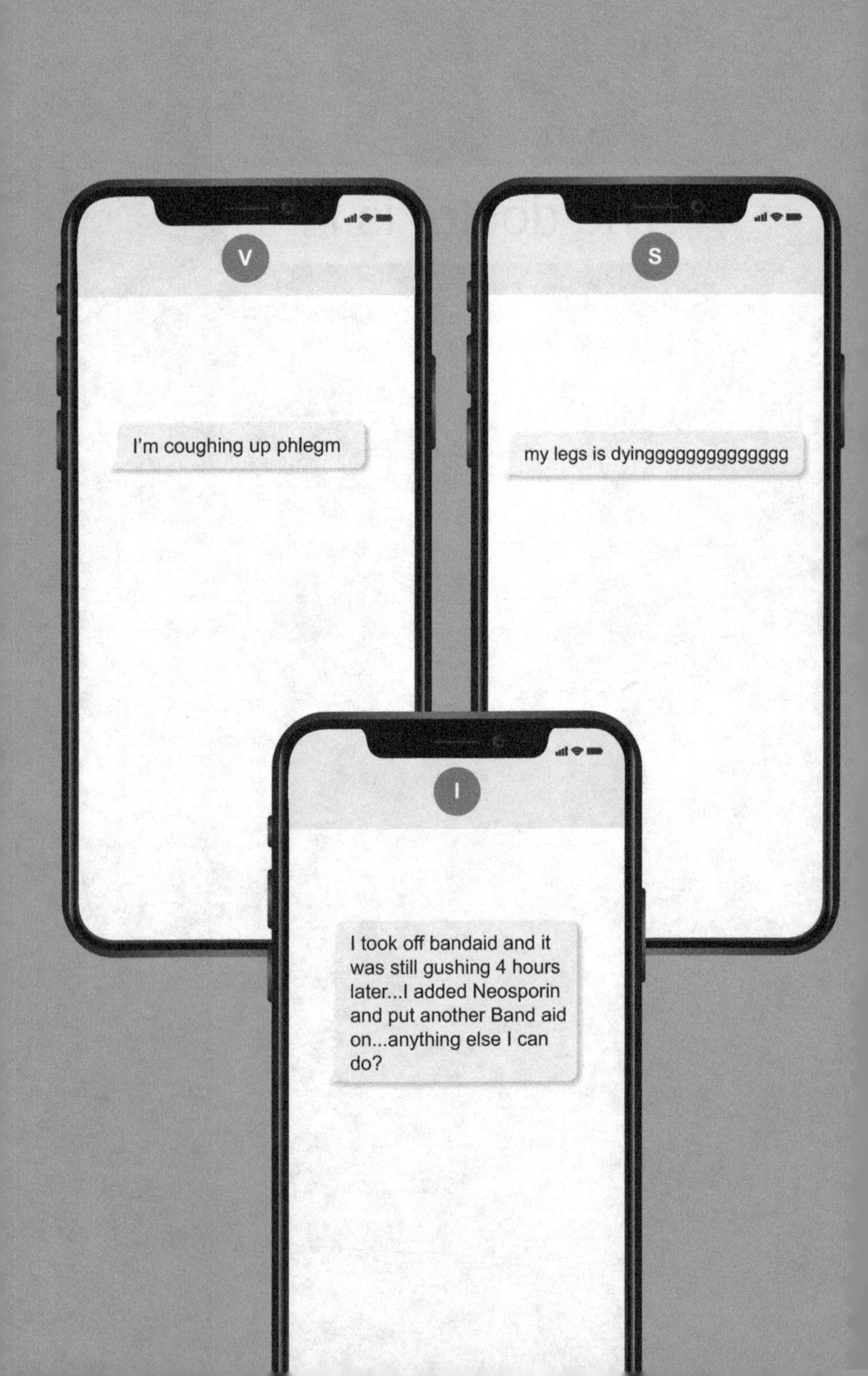
V
I'm coughing up phlegm
S
my legs is dyinggggggggggggg
I
I took off bandaid and it was still gushing 4 hours later...I added Neosporin and put another Band aid on...anything else I can do?

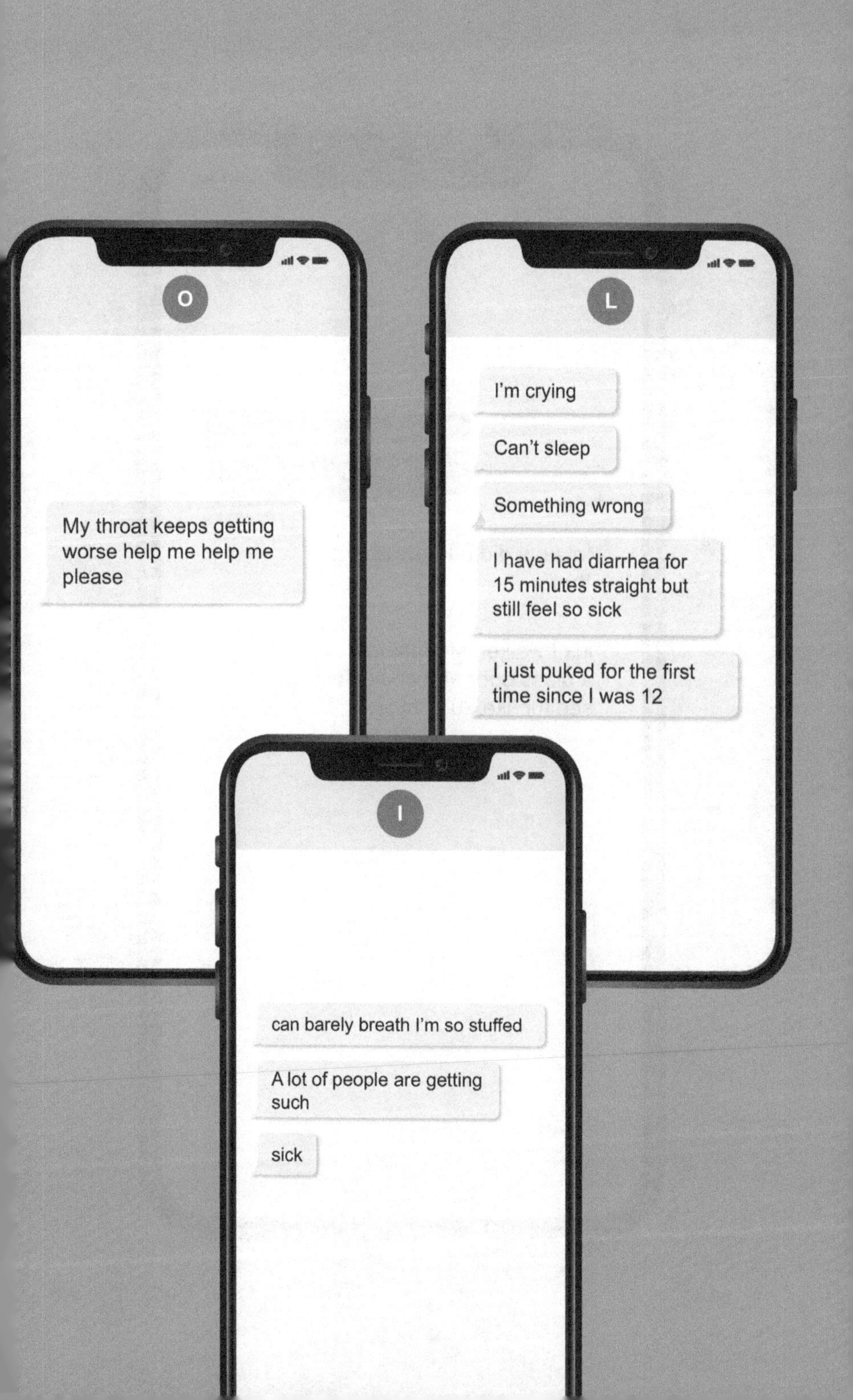
O
My throat keeps getting worse help me help me please
L
I'm crying
Can't sleep
Something wrong
I have had diarrhea for 15 minutes straight but still feel so sick
I just puked for the first time since I was 12
I
can barely breath I'm so stuffed
A lot of people are getting such
sick

Q
Do you think u really have a concussion
lol how did u know about that
idk I walked straight into a glass door and couldn't see for like 20 minutes

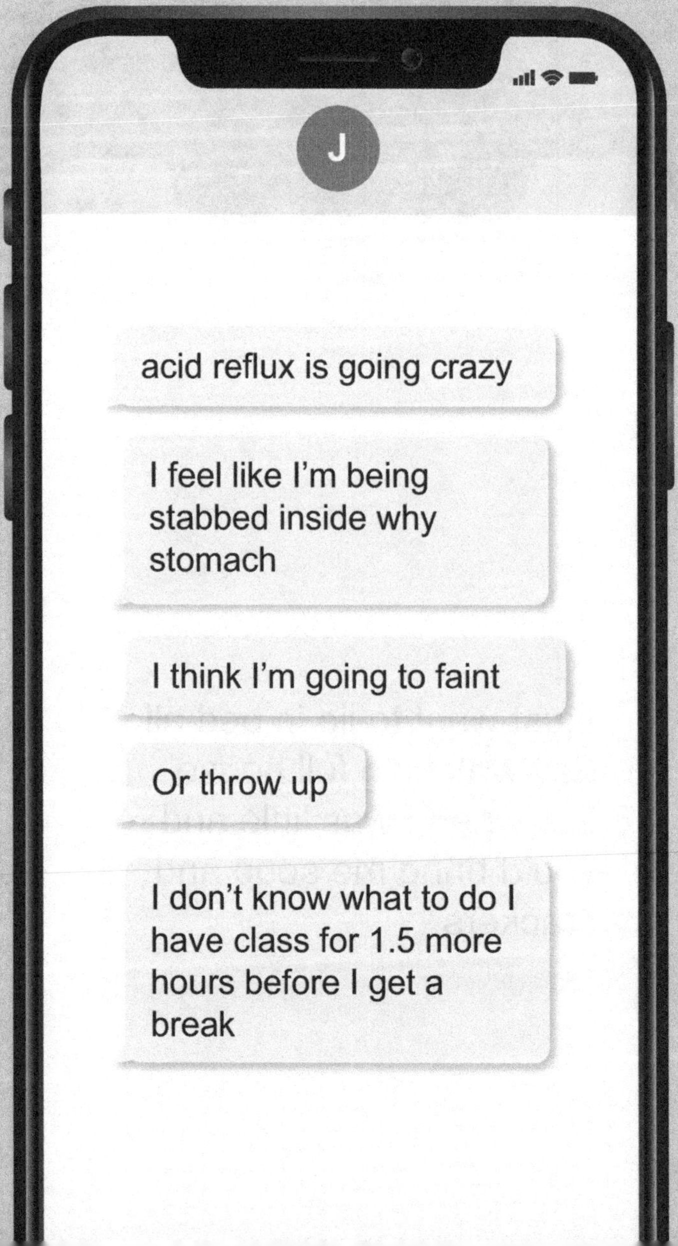

J

acid reflux is going crazy

I feel like I'm being stabbed inside why stomach

I think I'm going to faint

Or throw up

I don't know what to do I have class for 1.5 more hours before I get a break

T
I just want to lie in bed all day watching full house like when I was little and you'd bring me soup and crackers

K

I’m super sick from something I ate

I took pepto bismal

But what else do I do?

poor baby

It literally came out of my nose

Get clear Gatorade

H
Treda
BONADOXINA
You think it's ok I took the medicine right
Z
Idk if I should call out of work to go
If you feel it's bad enough go
I don't know
that's my mouth

D

Can I microwave a dish towel to make it hot? the doctor told me to make a hot compress as hot as I can handle

P

So I did just accidentally use a clorox wipe on my butt

what do i do

Use soap and water and wash really well

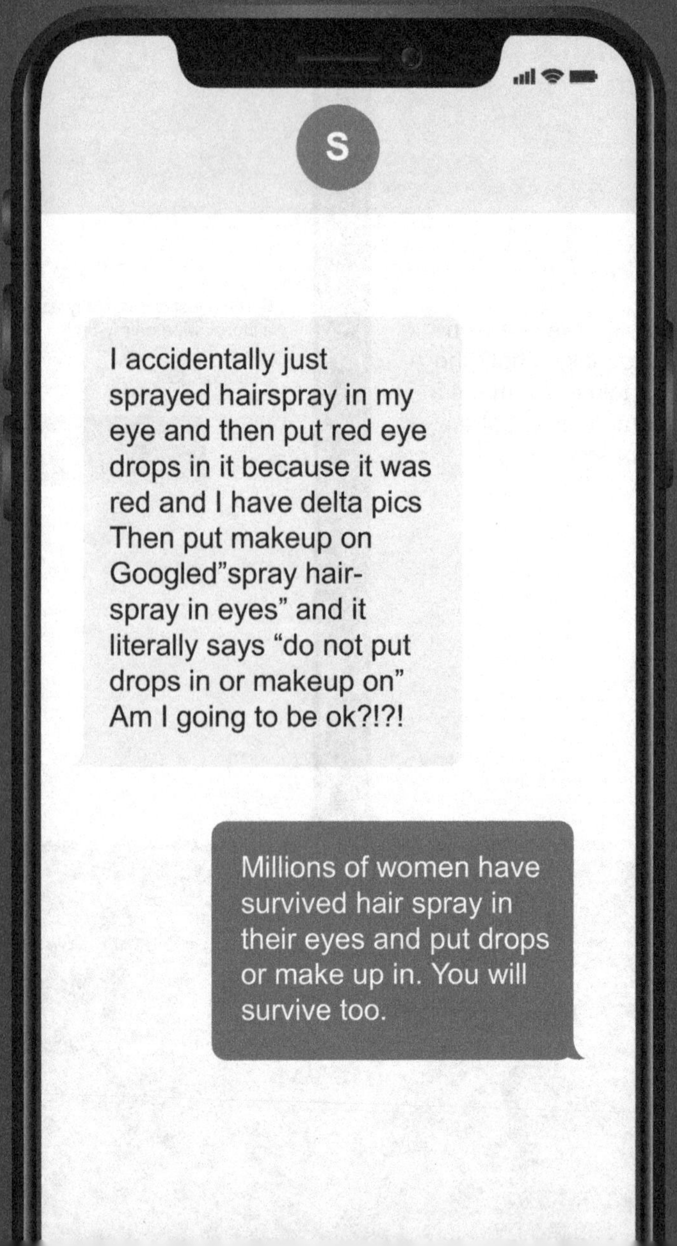

S

I accidentally just sprayed hairspray in my eye and then put red eye drops in it because it was red and I have delta pics Then put makeup on Googled"spray hair-spray in eyes" and it literally says "do not put drops in or makeup on" Am I going to be ok?!?!

Millions of women have survived hair spray in their eyes and put drops or make up in. You will survive too.

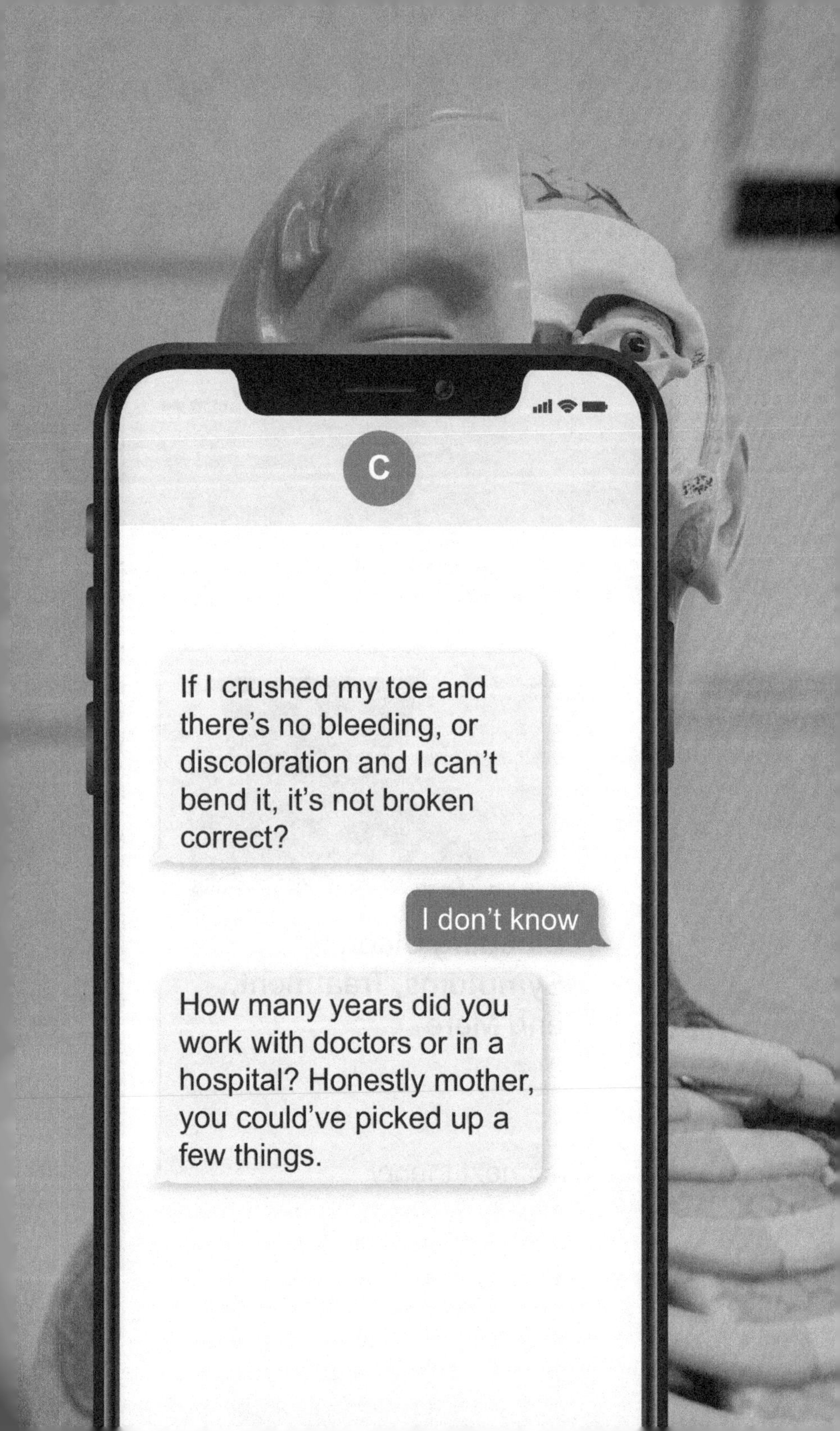
C
If I crushed my toe and there's no bleeding, or discoloration and I can't bend it, it's not broken correct?
I don't know
How many years did you work with doctors or in a hospital? Honestly mother, you could've picked up a few things.

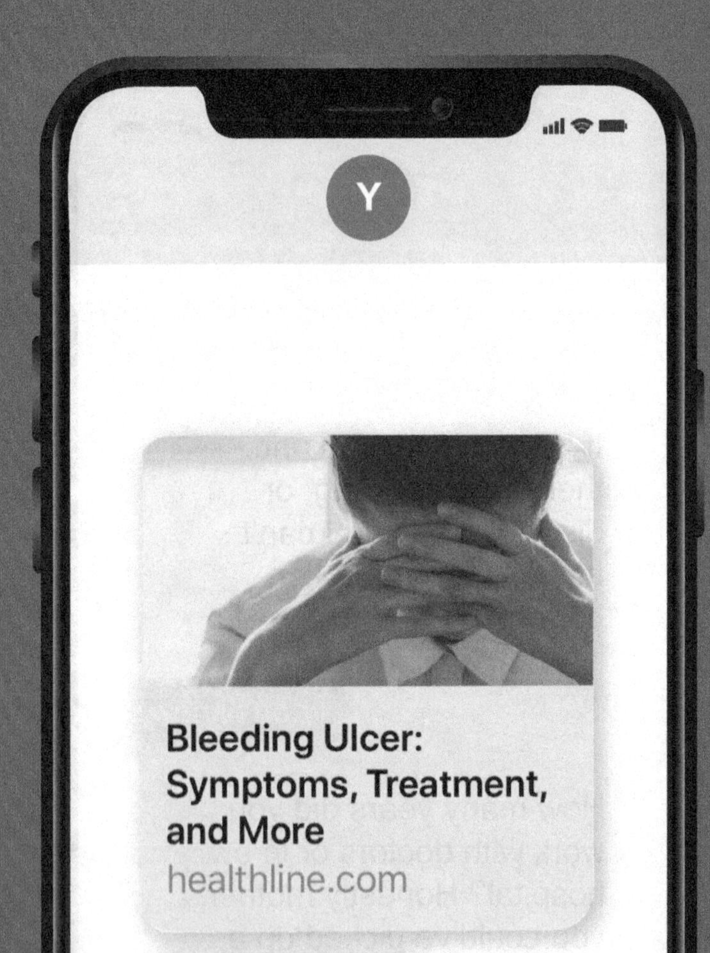
Y
Bleeding Ulcer: Symptoms, Treatment, and More
healthline.com
my next theory

R

10 Signs and Symptoms of Iron Deficiency

1. **Unusual** Tiredness. Share on Pinterest. ...
2. Paleness. **Pale skin** and **pale** coloring of the inside of the lower eyelids are other common **signs** of iron deficiency (5, 6, 7). ...
3. **Shortness of Breath**. ...
4. **Headaches** and **Dizziness**. ...
5. **Heart Palpitations**. ...
6. Dry and Damaged Hair and Skin. ...
7. Swelling and Soreness of the Tongue and Mouth. ...
8. Restless **Legs**.

I'm going blind too

H

Just took a bug out of my eye that has been there for 4 hours!

Lovely. Thanks for sharing!

ofc!

P
Have I gotten a flu shot?

D

What does our insurance cover

Like an MRI

Or just like normal stuff

It cover most anything a doctor would recommend. Nothing experimental or too new. Why?

What do you need a MRI for?

P

and I am going to get my flu shot later today

ok, glad it worked out and good idea

Germs pass quickly in dorms, so extra protection good!

Yep!

I’m debating if being an adult means I have to go buy my own post flu shot gelato

Cause I really feel like adults still need post vaccine dessert

Yes, yes they do

CHAPTER 6

Did they really just text that?

You truly can't make this stuff up. Bizarre? Ironic? Comically coincidental? Some texts are so unbelievable you just have to say, "did my child really just text that?"

L

didn't i die as a baby

and come back to life

obviously not

????

when i fell off the table and hit my head and stopped breathing?

you fell off a high counter and hit your head on a concrete floor and passed out/were unconscious for about 10 seconds

R

Hey buddy. Love you. How was your day?

We forgot to bring me a towel

Oh crap. Is there a CVS or Walgreens pharmacy that you can buy one?

No it's fine I found out how to dry off

How?

By standing in front of the fan acting like I'm on the front of the titanic

I literally snotted

Did I call you yesterday crying, too? Or was that the day before?

Ummm I’ve lost count??

I can’t remember I know I called you yesterday but I can’t remember if I cried or not lol

B

Can I get laser hair removal?

It's hard to get bikini waxes here

Z

Mouse over image for close-up

Stella Rosa Pink (750ml)

3 reviews

will you send me a bottle of this? or two?

No

S

When did Jen and Grant get married?

Oct 1988

And how long had they been dating?

Sorry I'm trying to plan my life

Careful or this will end up on my Instagram story

You'll have to ask Jen how long they dated

F
Mom, I have a shopping problem.

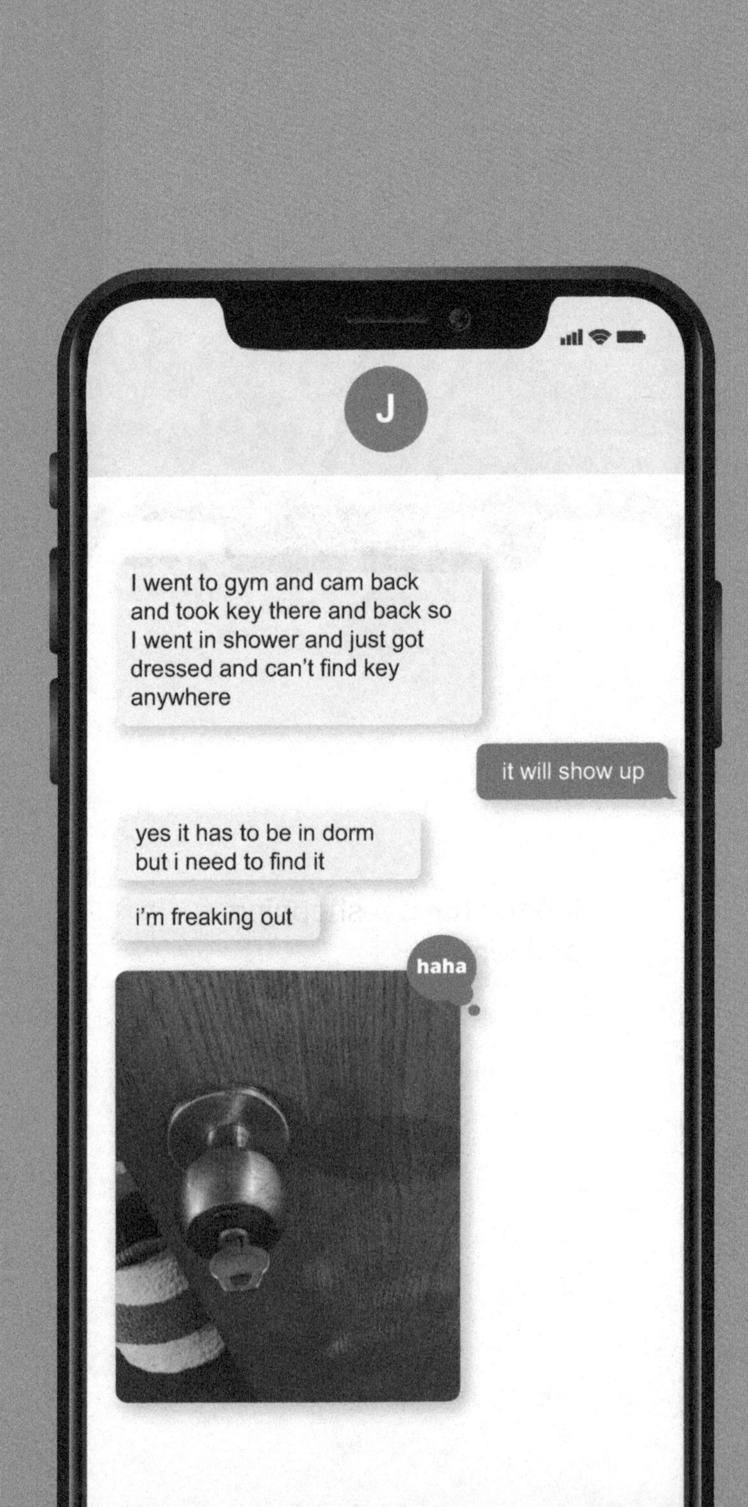
J
I went to gym and cam back and took key there and back so I went in shower and just got dressed and can't find key anywhere
it will show up
yes it has to be in dorm but i need to find it
i'm freaking out
haha

Y
Ok, I will. Thank you!
Also, I see a charge of 50-something to the Humane Society. Did you get a cat?
Uhhhh yeah so about that....

Saturday

I’ve been thinking about piercing my nose again. I don’t wanna do it if you’re gonna hate it again.... thoughts please

Today

Hey

Sup

I pierced my nose

H

Momma can I borrow $600?

No

T

I forgot where are we staying in Mexico

like what it’s called

I’m bored and want to look at pics

in class

shouldn’tt you be taking notes?

O
I may possibly take a little
Take a little what?
Mother. A sorority little. A child.

M
Baby
Babe
Babe
Babe
Babe
Hello?
Wrong chat
I'm your mother

C

I just won the knockout challenge

You're the bomb.com

How many people?

Do u get free tuition now?

like 30 i got a free domino's pizza. and then me and bo just won the 3 point contest

So no free tuition right?

another pizza

E

I'm locked between the bathroom and the door in my towel

huh?

It's hard to explain

I don't get it. What will you do?

I'm not sure!

Made it!

Phew

S
What do you wear for a Miami Vice theme? What even is that?
80's?

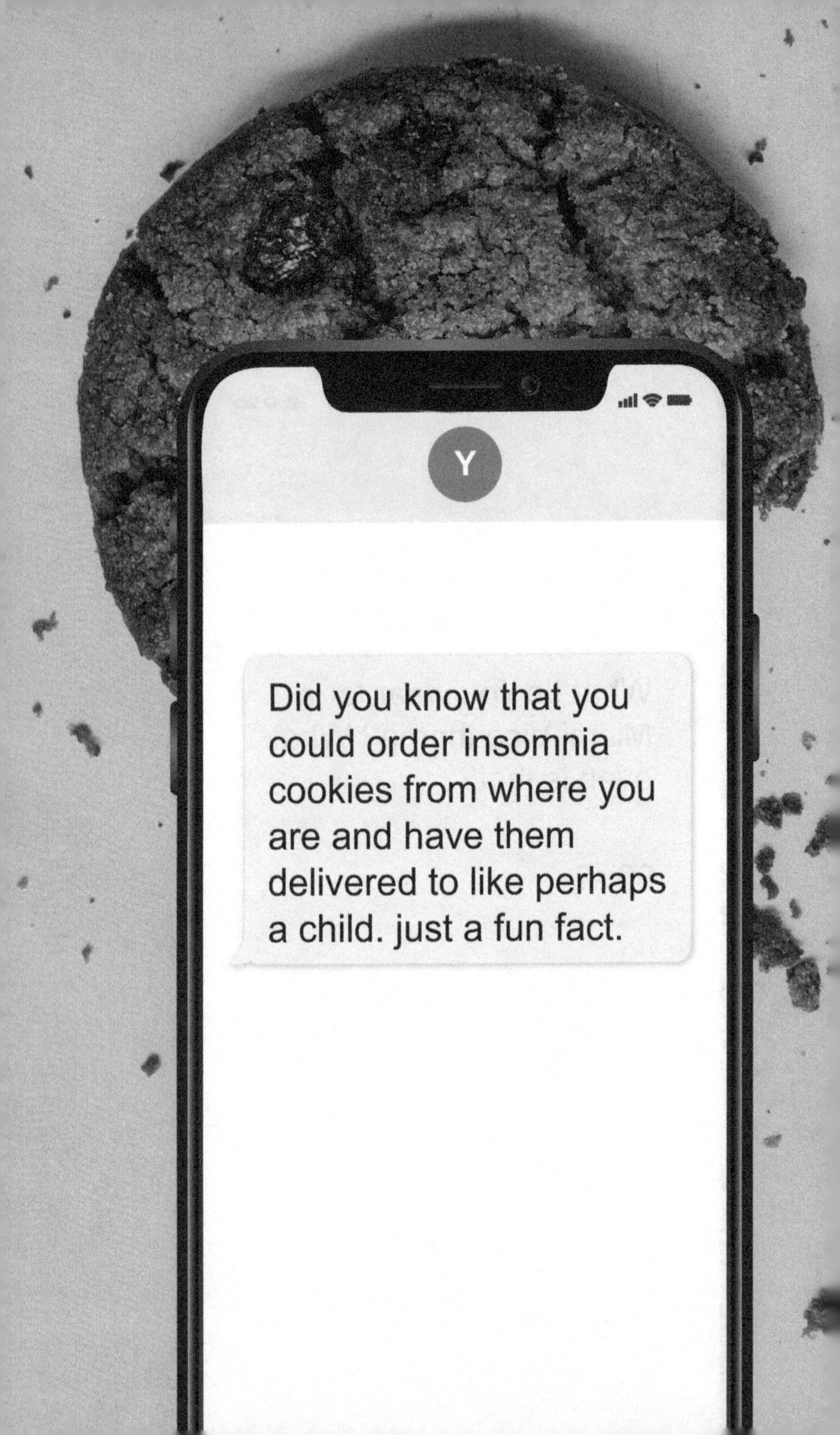
Y
Did you know that you could order insomnia cookies from where you are and have them delivered to like perhaps a child. just a fun fact.

W

Bird just pooped on my hands

at least someone is pooping

Gross. That's good luck

swag money

Adulting is hard

There's a lot more to college than showing up to class. Managing finances, securing summer internships, voting and mailing letters are just a few of the immense responsibilities "burdening" college students.

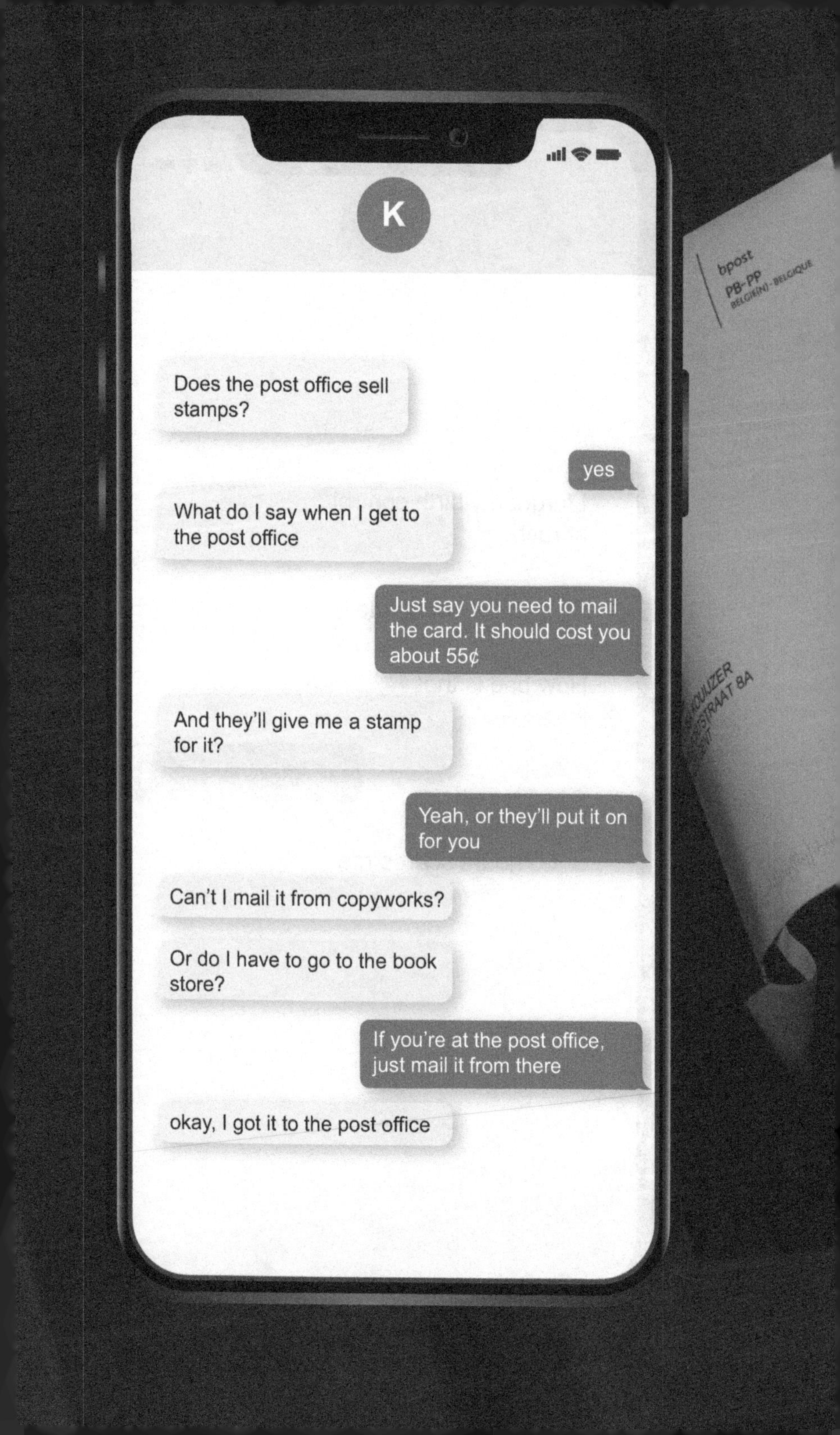

K

Does the post office sell stamps?

yes

What do I say when I get to the post office

Just say you need to mail the card. It should cost you about 55¢

And they'll give me a stamp for it?

Yeah, or they'll put it on for you

Can't I mail it from copyworks?

Or do I have to go to the book store?

If you're at the post office, just mail it from there

okay, I got it to the post office

bpost
PB-PP
BELGIE(N) - BELGIQUE

N
I forgot my birth control at rush
So I'll be 3 hours late
How bad is that
You know it's fine
But 3 hours scares me

P
What's the weather in Colorado? I wanna know what to pack?
Seriously. You have the same iPhone I have

H

I'm never drinking again

That hung over?

yes

Throwing up?

Yes but throwing up nothing

I'm fine now

What did you drink?

Tequila

Voicemail

(313) 923-3087
unknown
November 28, 2018 at 5:39 PM

Transcription Beta
"This is Sarah calling with Amazon ________ word we need people in your area to work with Amazon from home starting paid $27.50 an hour sign up an Amazon ________ ____________ profits.org..."

Was this transcription **useful** or **not useful**?

0:13 -0:01

Audio Call Back Delete

(734) 201-1349 Yesterday
unknown 0:05

should I look into this

No - do NOT trust that!

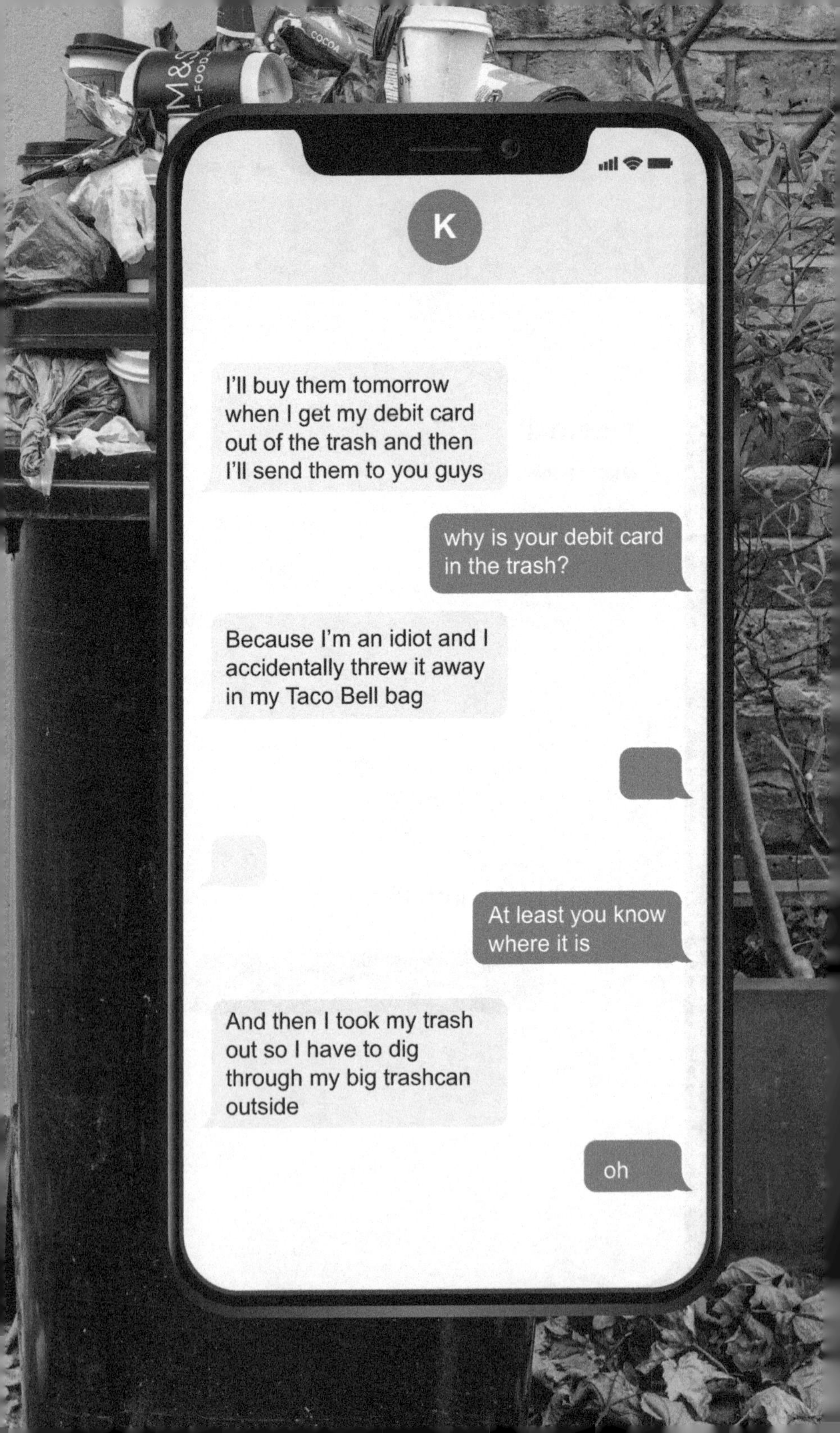
K
I'll buy them tomorrow when I get my debit card out of the trash and then I'll send them to you guys
why is your debit card in the trash?
Because I'm an idiot and I accidentally threw it away in my Taco Bell bag
At least you know where it is
And then I took my trash out so I have to dig through my big trashcan outside
oh

R

How do I void a check again?

Write VOID in big letters on it

Really?

Yes

CHAPTER 8

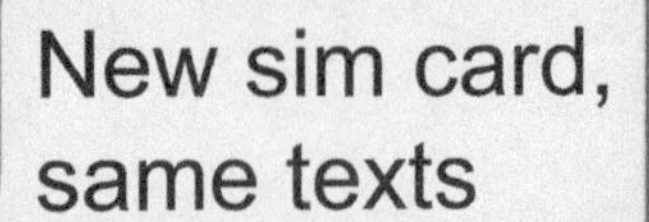

New sim card, same texts

Nearly 1 in 10 American students study abroad as undergraduates. Often, they live with host families and take all their classes in a second language.

Typically, they travel to multiple countries, successfully navigating foreign currency, train schedules, youth hostels and visa requirements. And yet, they still text from 4,000 miles away for help.

Saw rocks. So cold.

L
You never answered me. I am assuming you left alreadt? Lol
We just left
We had to hike down the snowy mountain
wow.
It was a mess. They called the national guard to get us down but we just decided to hike
That's crazy

A

RUBY MURRAY

MATTAR PANEER

A steadfast and humble vegetarian curry, the sort that can be found in any good Indian roadside restaurant. (V) 9.50

CHICKEN RUBY

A good and proper curry redolent with spice and flavour. Tender chicken in a rich silky 'makhani' sauce, best mopped up with a Roomali Roti. 10.50

SLIP-DISC: DISHOOM'S BOMBAY LONDON GROOVES

would I like chicken ruby?

Q

Hi there is a tarantula in my room

Not sure what I can do about it from NY but can someone help you deal with that NOW

Is it really a tarantula or just a spider?

It's called a huntsman spider

And it's huge

Can you kill it?

Or can someone kill it?

We lost it

It disappeared

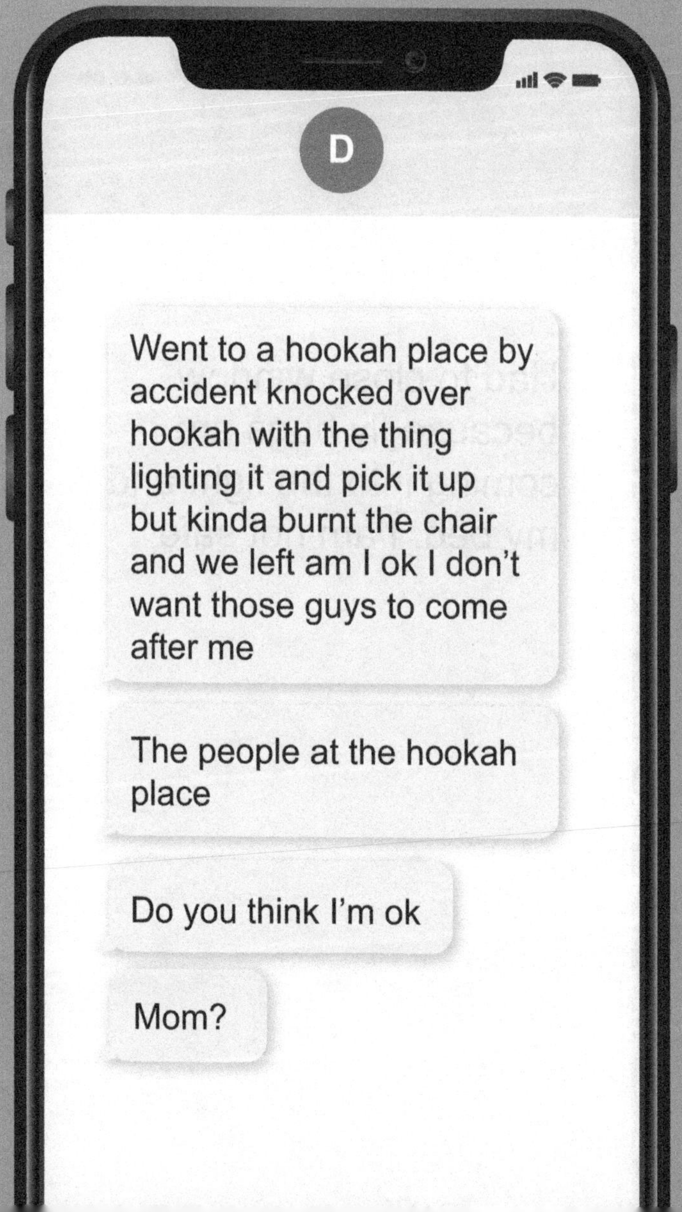

D

Went to a hookah place by accident knocked over hookah with the thing lighting it and pick it up but kinda burnt the chair and we left am I ok I don't want those guys to come after me

The people at the hookah place

Do you think I'm ok

Mom?

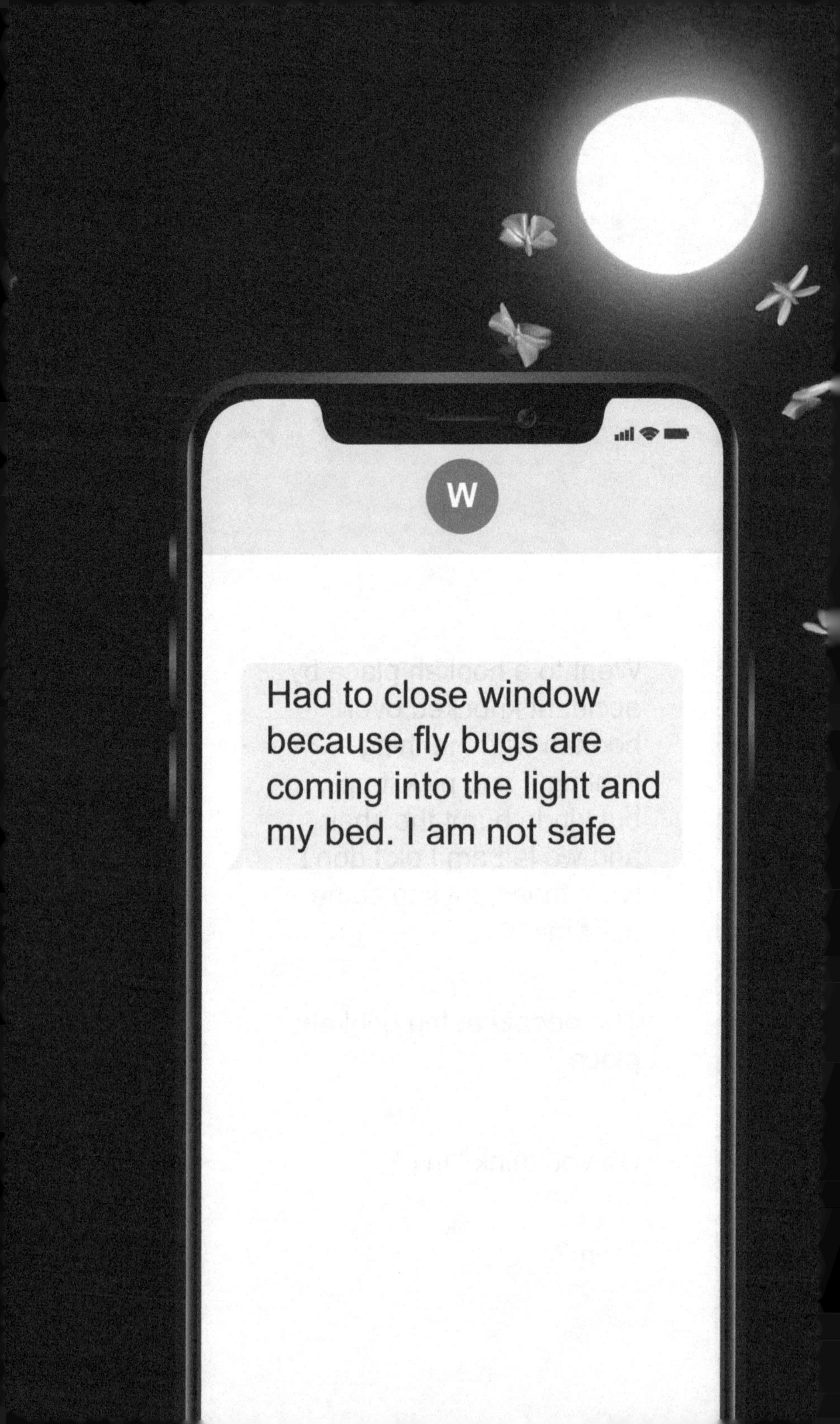
W
Had to close window because fly bugs are coming into the light and my bed. I am not safe

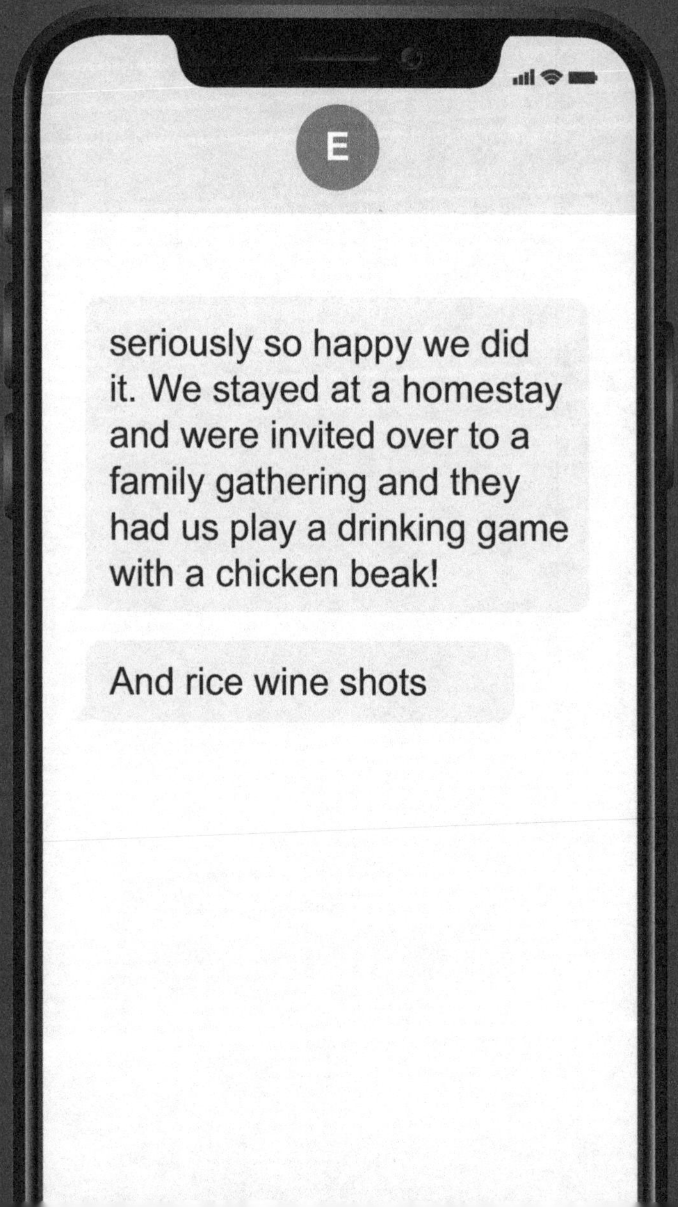

E

seriously so happy we did it. We stayed at a homestay and were invited over to a family gathering and they had us play a drinking game with a chicken beak!

And rice wine shots

CHAPTER 9

Life's not fair

Texting offers a safe outlet to VENT life's injustices. College students don't text because they want us to solve their problems. College students aren't necessarily interested in our opinions or advice. College students do want us to know that "the struggle is real".

Z

Been stopped for a while

Middle of Nowehere

Can you call Amtrak and see what is going on?

The lights have one out

Call and fucking sue Amtrak this is unacceptable as business

The cabin is freezing outlets wont work unless the train is running

20-30 in each. Rather die

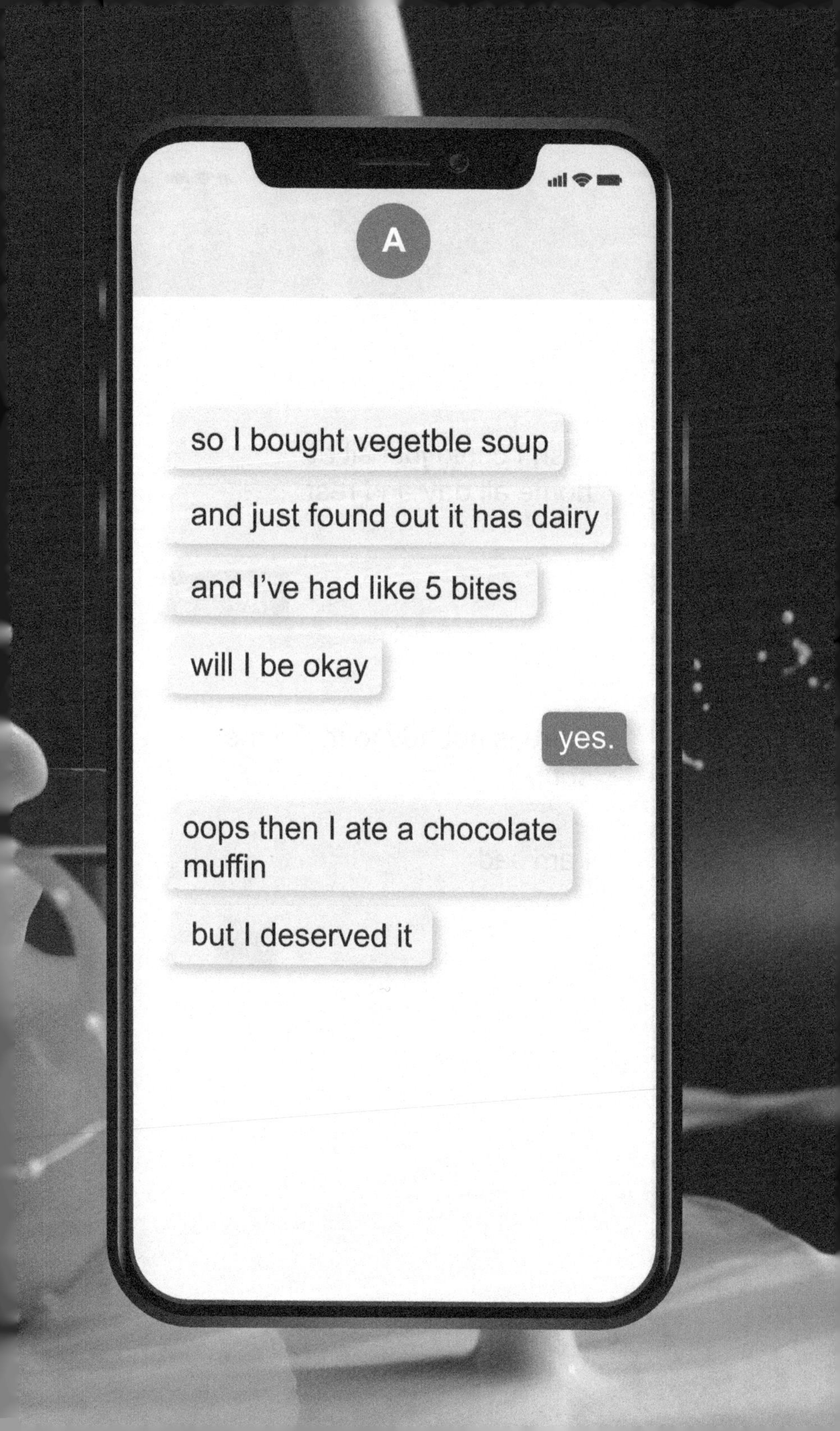

A

so I bought vegetble soup

and just found out it has dairy

and I've had like 5 bites

will I be okay

yes.

oops then I ate a chocolate muffin

but I deserved it

F

wish I could just sit at home all day and rest

me too

there is nobody to make me soup

I am sad

O
I'm too spoiled I keep thinking about how I'm gonna get used to having essentially free Starbucks at my fingertips whenever I want and then the transition to adulthood is gonna be soo disappointing
LOL

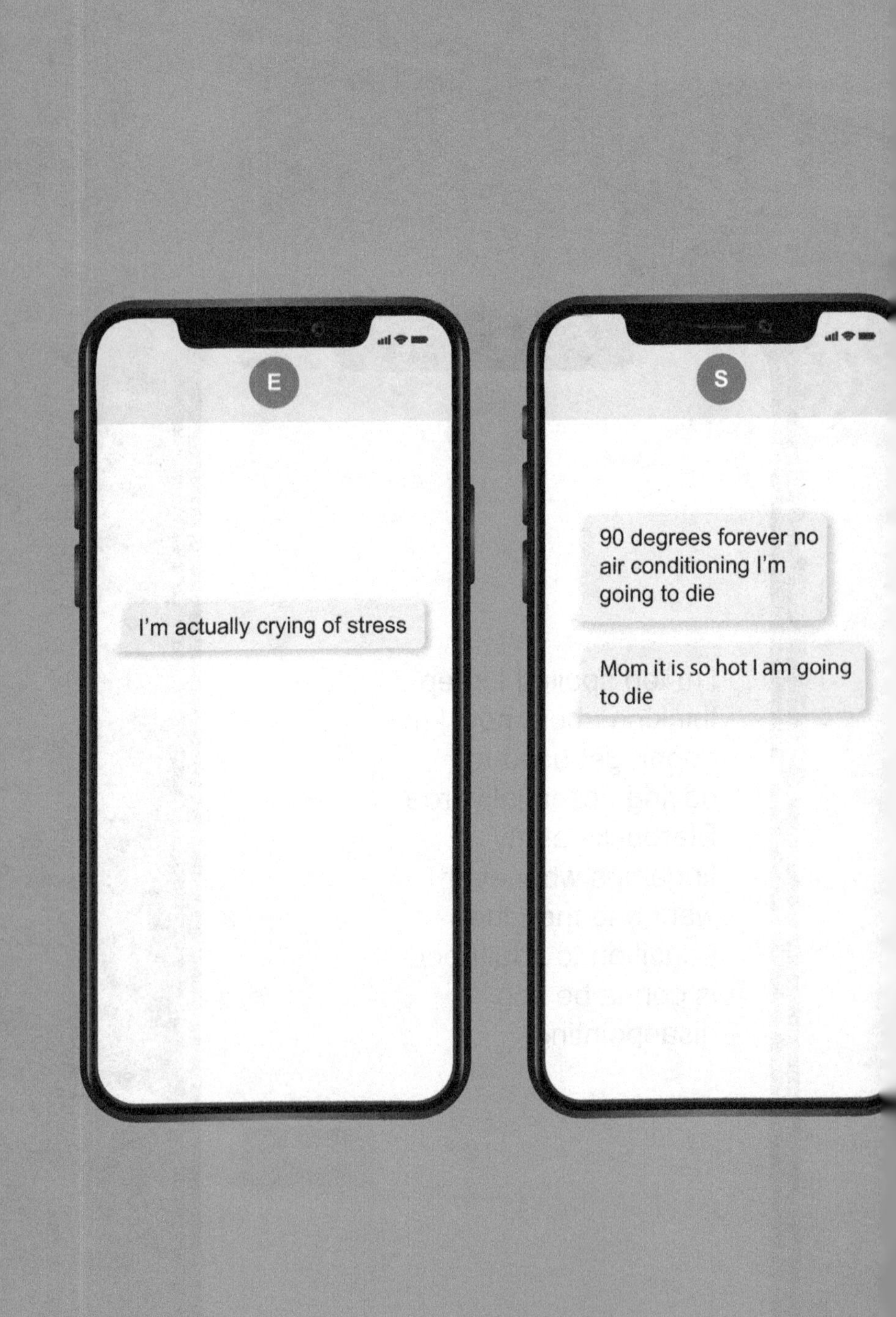
E
I'm actually crying of stress
S
90 degrees forever no air conditioning I'm going to die
Mom it is so hot I am going to die

Q
I'm dying
please do not text that and please do not do that!
I
Its 48 out
Come on!
Are you freezing
Death is upon me

V
Mom it’s so hot I’m going to die
S
90 degrees forever no air conditioning I’m going to die

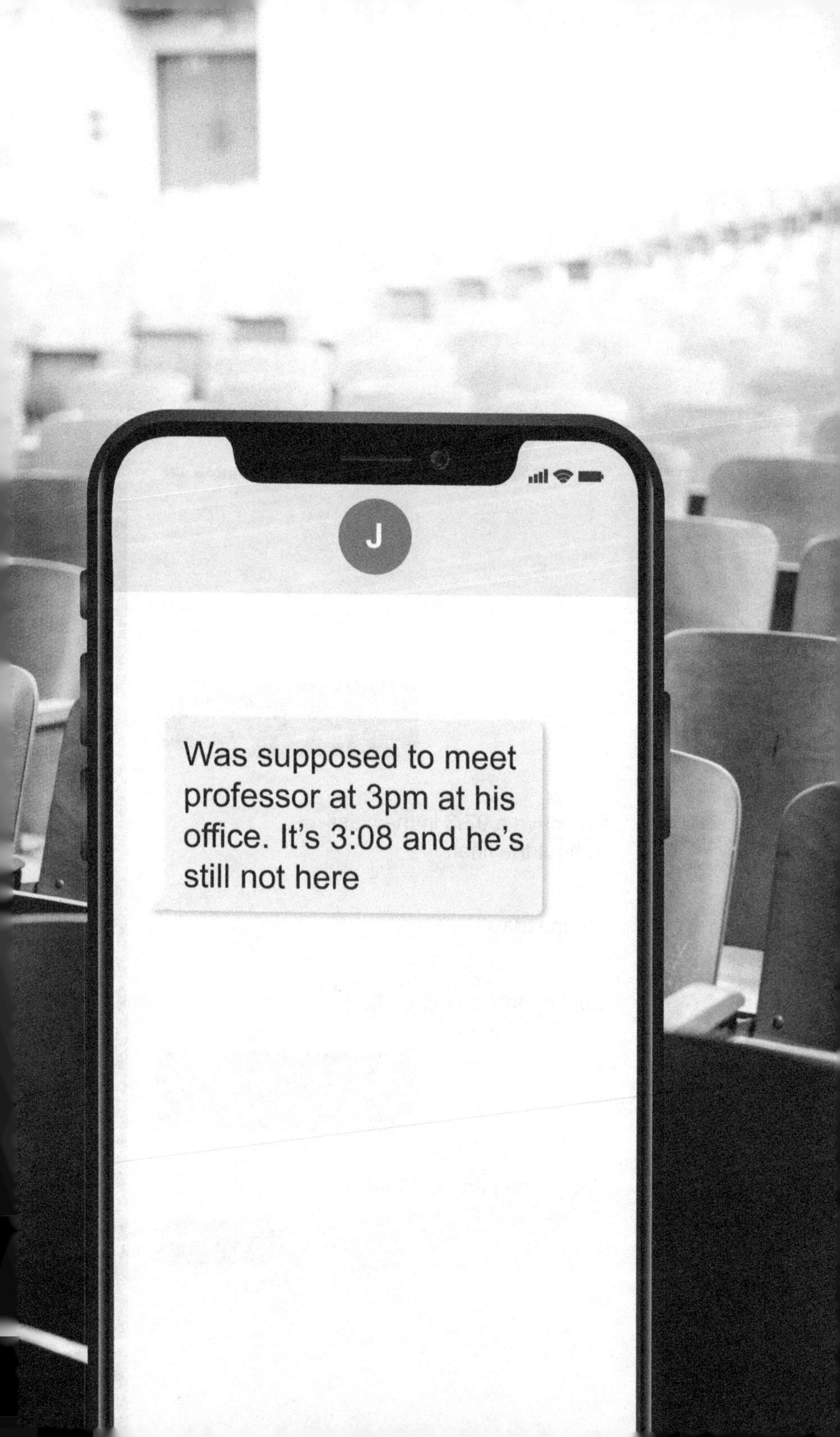
J
Was supposed to meet professor at 3pm at his office. It's 3:08 and he's still not here

R

Nice. When is your last class then

So I have a 97.3 in the class without the final

Wednesday

but I'm not leaving early

Why aren't you leaving. You don't like me?

I'm gonna party for 3 days

Oh great.

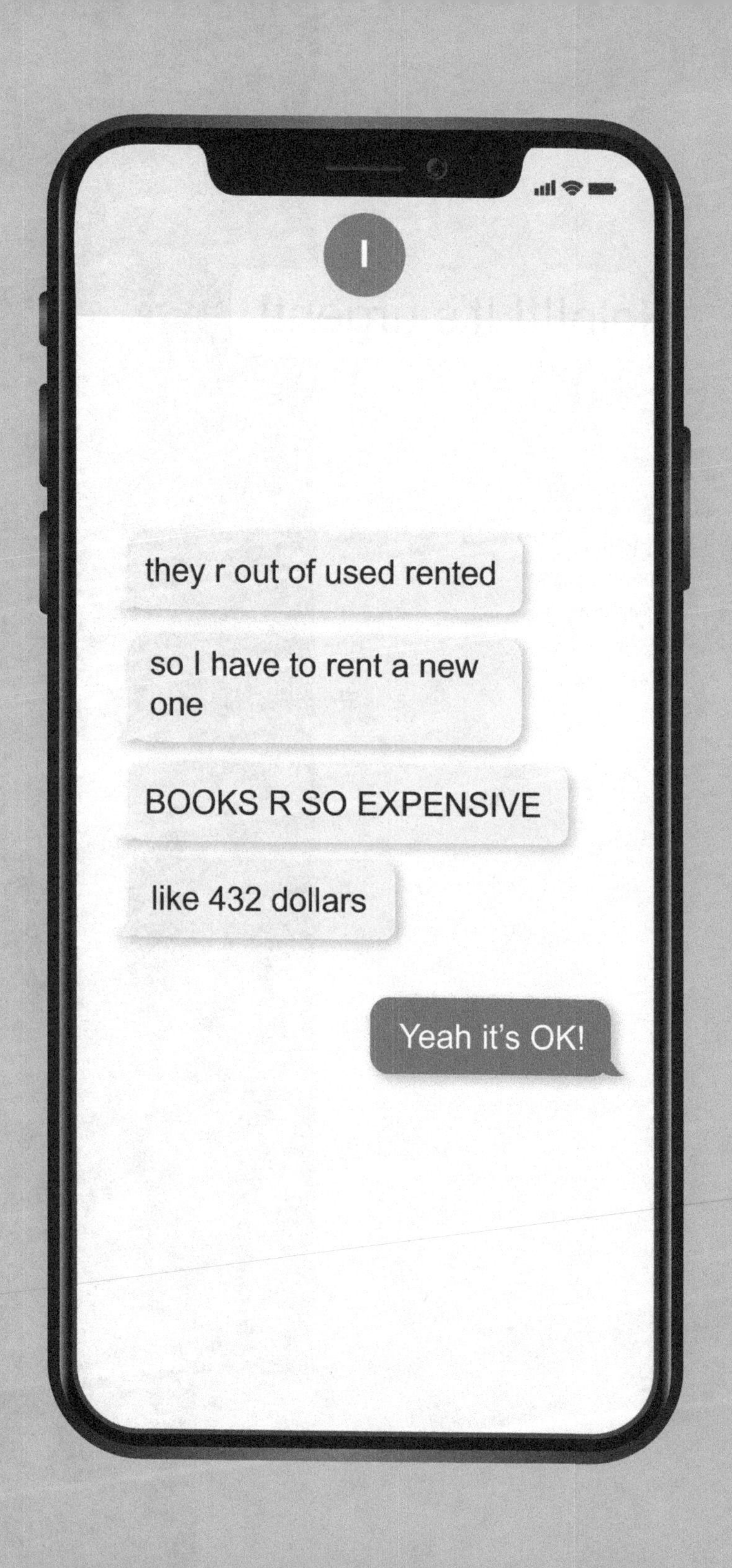
I
they r out of used rented
so I have to rent a new one
BOOKS R SO EXPENSIVE
like 432 dollars
Yeah it's OK!

CHAPTER 11

Help!!!! It's urgent!

Nothing like sitting in a meeting, hearing your phone vibrate and seeing

Hello????

MOM??

flash on your phone screen. What does it mean? These texts are code for: "I texted you 30 seconds ago, why haven't you answered?"

Our children are accustomed to instantaneous results. Need a ride? They get an Uber in a few minutes. Need a book? With Amazon Prime it arrives in a day. Have a question? Send a text.

Ironically, even as they expect that everyone should respond to their texts immediately, they establish clear parameters regarding when we should expect to receive responses to our texts.

IM HAVING A CRISIS

ik ur not still awake but pls tell me ur still awake

Today 6:07 AM

What is wrong

I was asleep

it's fine

i wanna change my major

R
MOM!!!!!!!!!
HELP!!!!!!!!
can I put my slippers in the dryer?

M
emergency
call
All the library cubicles are filled or locked
JOSE MARIA DE PEREDA - OBRAS - COMPLETAS II
JOSE MARIA DE PEREDA - OBRAS - COMPLETAS I
CALDERÓN DE LA BARCA OBRAS
EL EPIGRAMA ESPAÑOL
248
VICENTE ALEIXANDRE OBRAS COMPLETAS

S
Mom
I'm having an absolute crisis
I dropped. My mask. In the toilet
This is how it ends.
This is how I go out.
what am I supposed to do
The one I just got?
yes oh my god that is not the most important thing here!!!
Wash it in the sink
and then wear it???????
Really well
S
mom
wash it in the sink??????
I'm gonna throw up
oh god
what do I do
Mom
MOM
My brand new mask?
okay
I'm going to die
I'll meet you outside

S
This is the worst case scenario
I couldn't have imagined this going more poorly
I'm going to die
No, we will just leave
can you check out
You are amazing
and I'll meet you outside
I'll check out

C

I need my social securty

On the phone I need it

MOM

NOW

H

I'm really scared. I think I saw a ghost in my room last night

K

We miss you

miss you too now I’m trying to sleep

please text me after 9 from now on

sorry

CHAPTER 12

Just wanted to say

Simply said, every once in a while, we receive a frame worthy text!

THANK YOU.

K

Thank you for this weekend mama. I had such a good time and I missed you guys so much and I was so happy to be home. I really appreciate everything that you and daddy have given me. You guys mean everything to me and I can't thank you enough for all the love I have felt from you. It feels good to be back at school but I love and miss you all ♥

V
You raised me really well. I'm teaching all the other kids how to do everything
I think I'll get that tattooed
on my arm

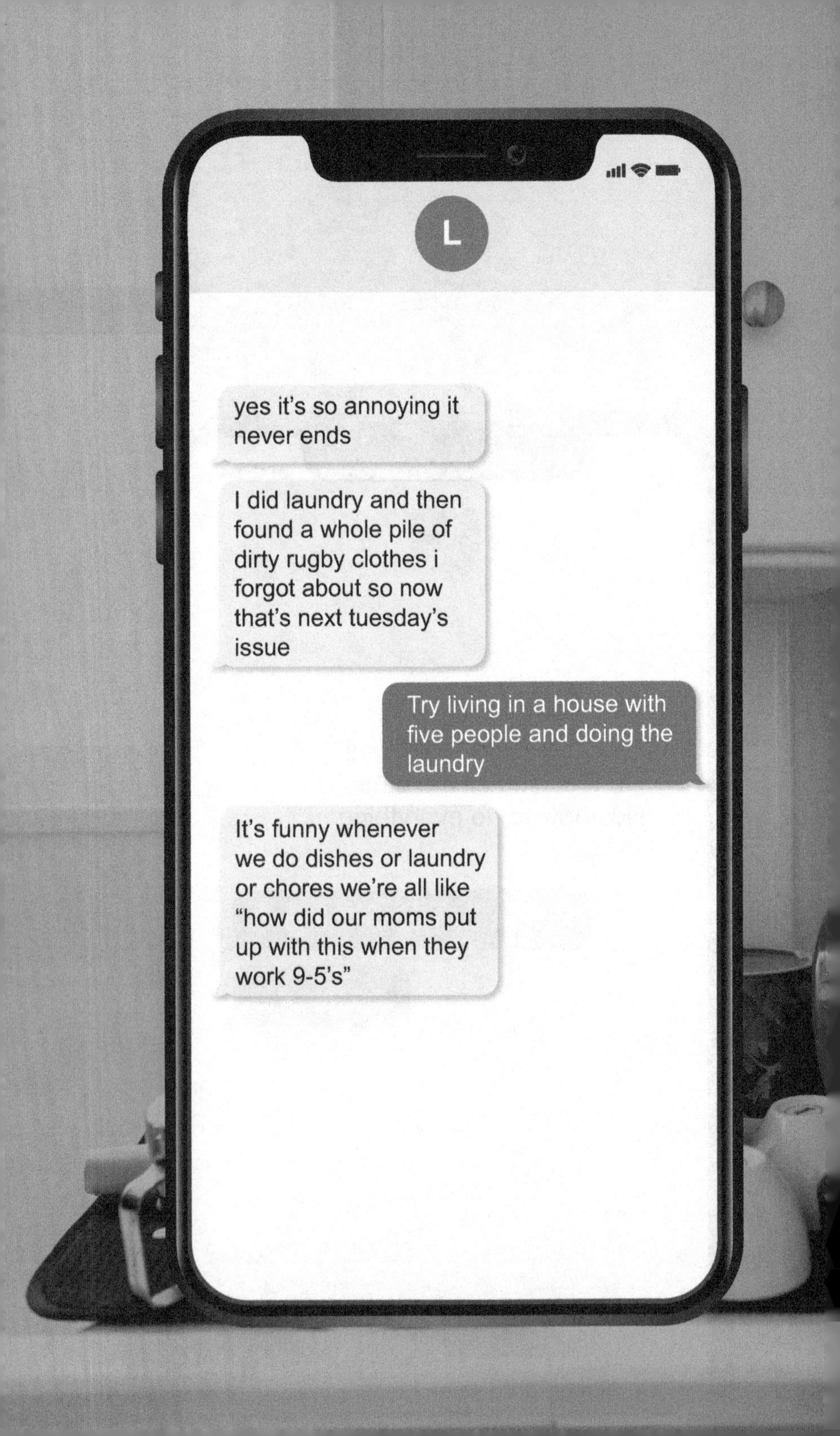
L
yes it's so annoying it never ends
I did laundry and then found a whole pile of dirty rugby clothes i forgot about so now that's next tuesday's issue
Try living in a house with five people and doing the laundry
It's funny whenever we do dishes or laundry or chores we're all like "how did our moms put up with this when they work 9-5's"

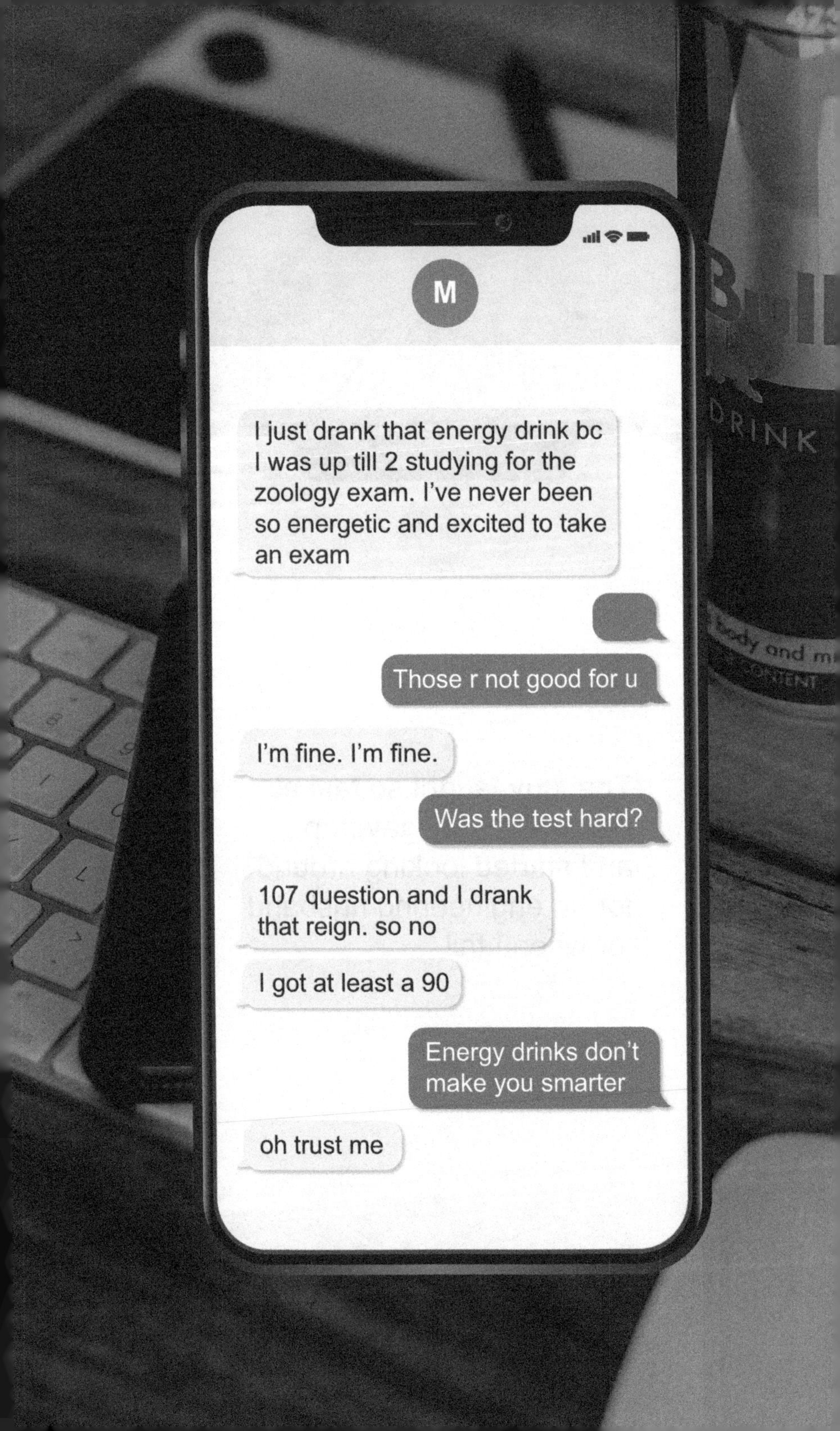
M
I just drank that energy drink bc I was up till 2 studying for the zoology exam. I've never been so energetic and excited to take an exam
Those r not good for u
I'm fine. I'm fine.
Was the test hard?
107 question and I drank that reign. so no
I got at least a 90
Energy drinks don't make you smarter
oh trust me
DRINK

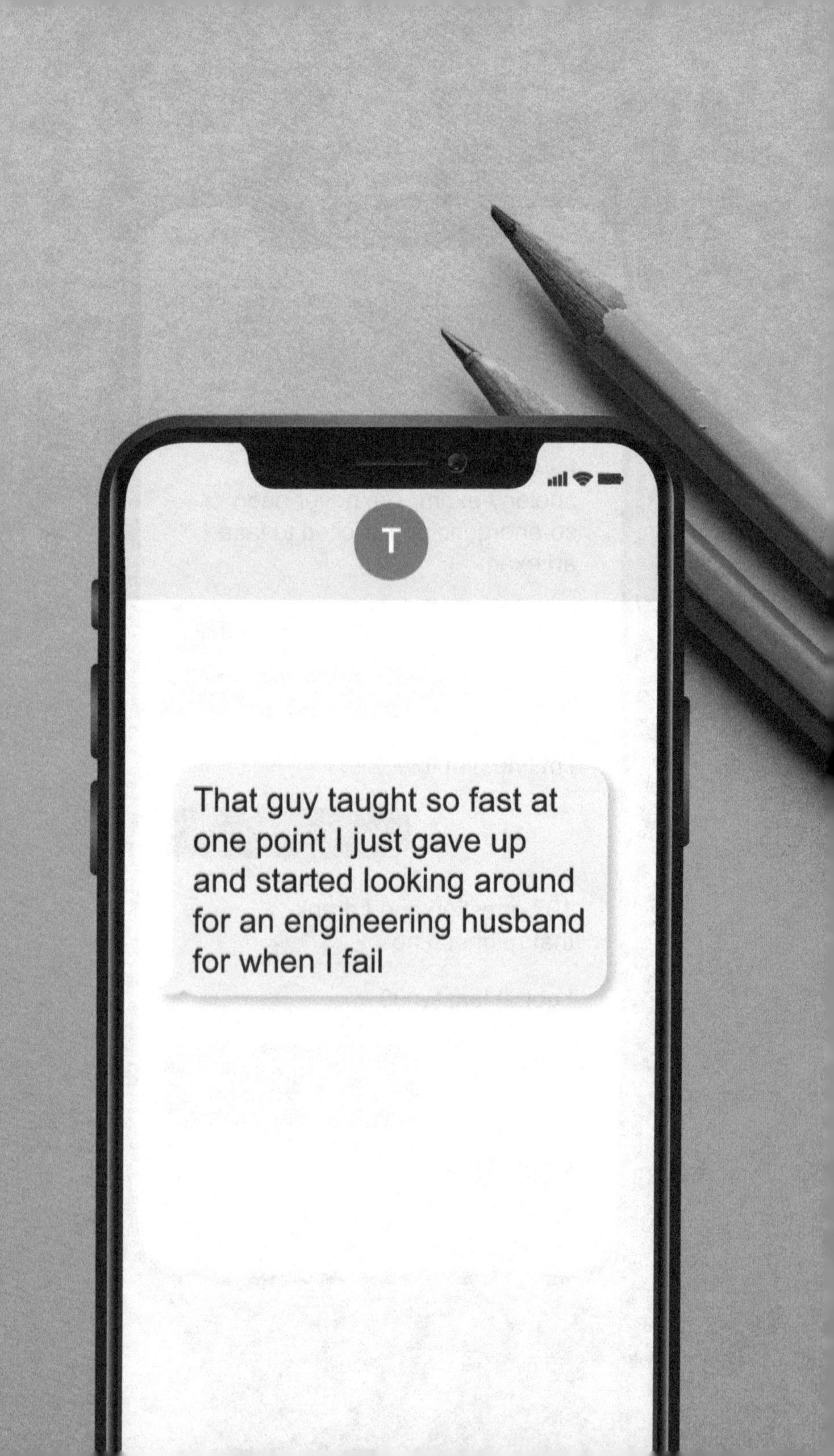
T
That guy taught so fast at one point I just gave up and started looking around for an engineering husband for when I fail

G
Do you think it would be bad if I dropped witchcraft?
I find it interesting. The class just takes SO much time and it's just extra credits that I don't need but at the same time it is really interesting and I know I'm here to learn.

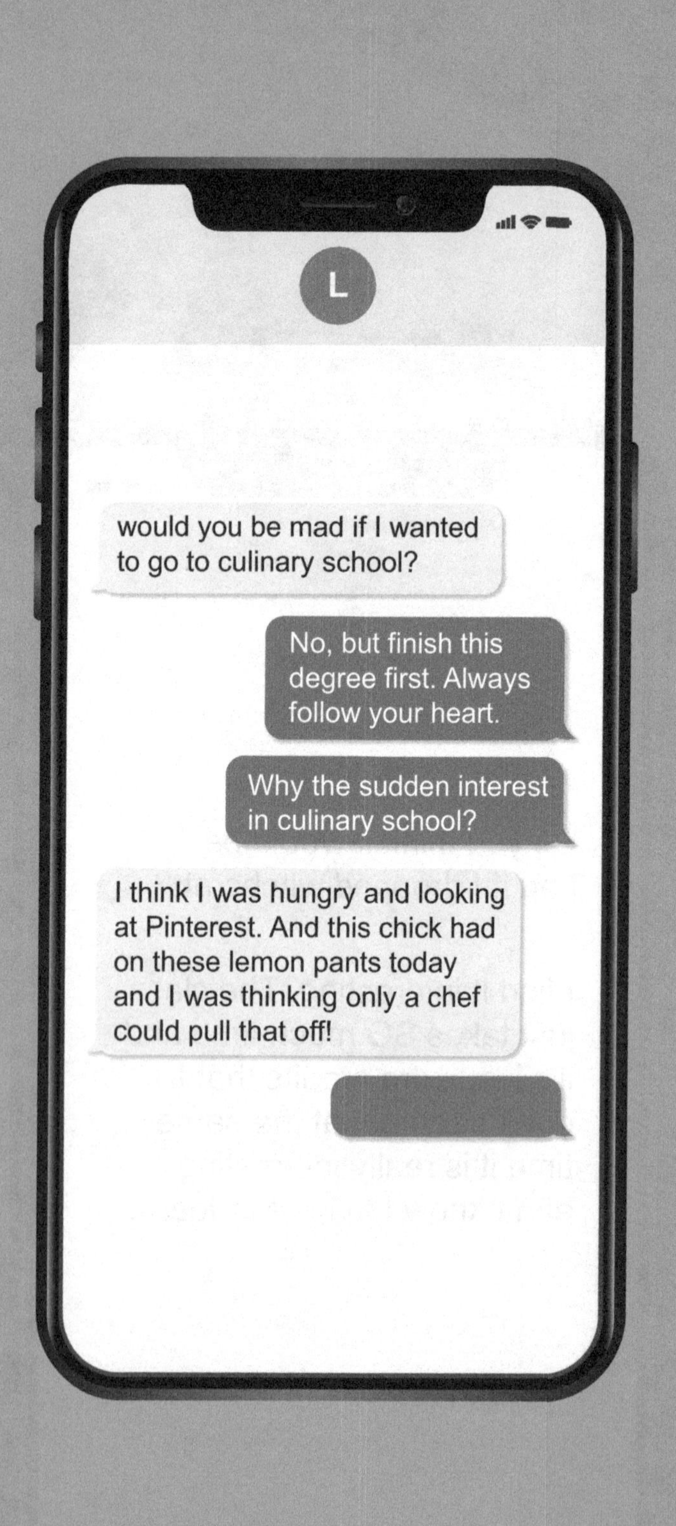
L
would you be mad if I wanted to go to culinary school?
No, but finish this degree first. Always follow your heart.
Why the sudden interest in culinary school?
I think I was hungry and looking at Pinterest. And this chick had on these lemon pants today and I was thinking only a chef could pull that off!

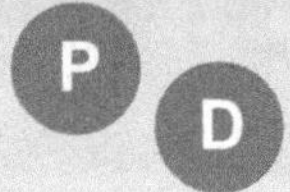

P

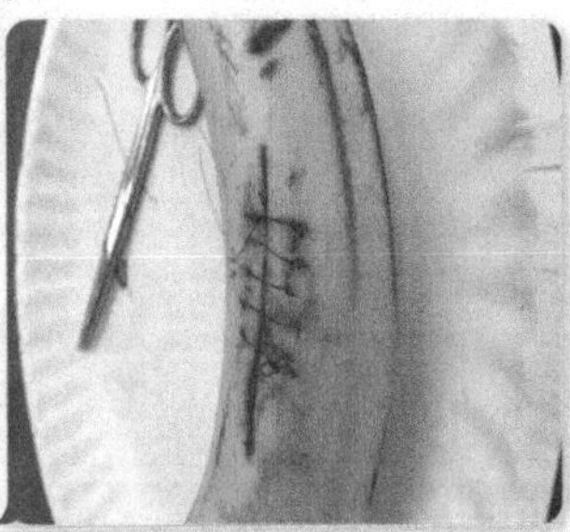

How do you like my stitches?

Wow, that's pretty good. I would even let you stitch me up!

P

I went to a suture clinic tonight, it was really cool.

By the way, it was run by the Army. I'm kinda interested

WTF?? The Army? Do you have any idea what is involved with that?

Call me!!!! What the hell!!!!!

Dad

Awesome. They will pay for medical school.

CHAPTER 10

Yes, there are classes here too

Of all the texts submitted for this book, less than a handful related to academics or professors and only a few were particularly noteworthy. Perhaps this is good news.

Our children are so well prepared for college that academics are not a source of stress or frustration.

Or perhaps it's just an indication of priorities - what do you think?

H

Also, can I take a second to apologize to you?

Um, yeah?

For what?

For never changing out the gosh darn toilet paper... I mean seriously, I never realized how actually frusterating it is to be the ONLY ONE in the dorm to change it out! How FREAKING HARD is it to reach over, grab the paper and switch out the roll... You don't even have to stand up

I love this so much

And don't get me STARTED on turning off the light when we leave the room.

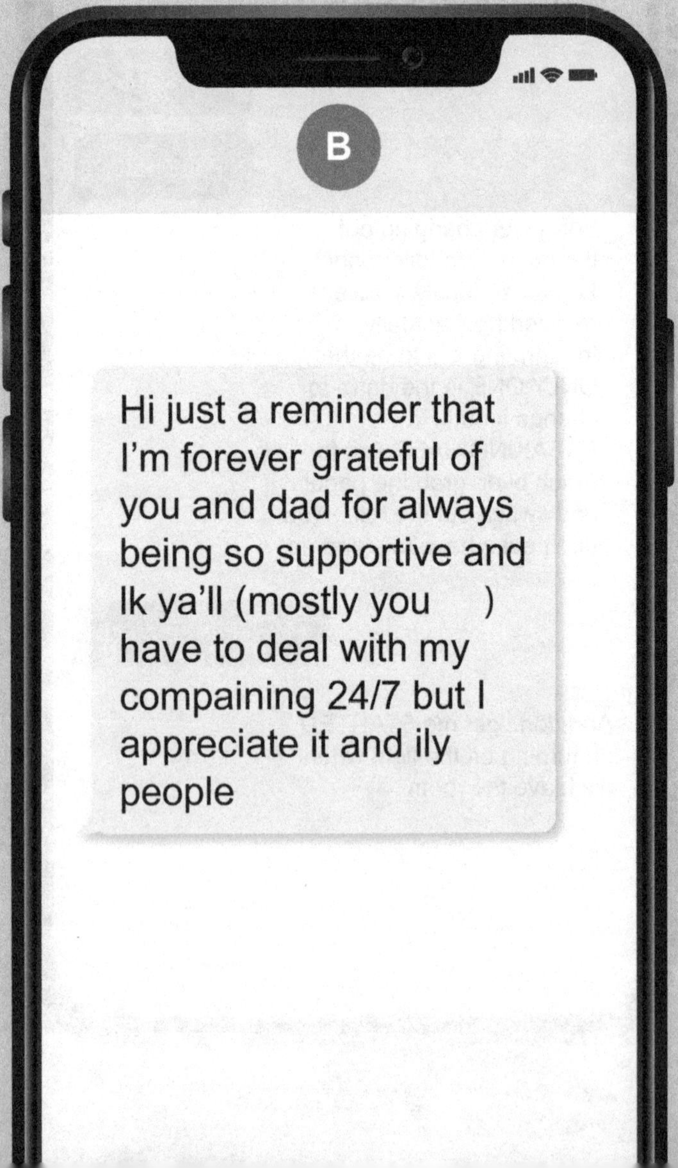

B

Hi just a reminder that I'm forever grateful of you and dad for always being so supportive and Ik ya'll (mostly you) have to deal with my compaining 24/7 but I appreciate it and ily people

A
Hey baby are you okay
Yes mom lol
I 🖤 you princesses 👸
I didn't die mom
I just haven't called you today

W

I didn't realize how hard it is to find a pillow that is comfortable????? You have been picking & providing my pillows my whole life, so now that my pillow from home was murdered in the dryer, I sadly am on an endless hunt to that my neck doesn't hurt so thank you for always somehow knowing what pillows are good!!!!!! Lol

E
Good
How are you?
What's up?
I just wanted to know what you were doing
I was just about to start loading the dishwasher.
I feel like I've been busy recently and haven't really talked to you
I know

J

It was a lot of fun too

I can imagine. The pictures I saw of you, it looked like you were enjoying yourself. I am so glad to hear.

Keep it up and keep working hard.

I will! And thank you!

I'm proud of you so. Great job, and keep enjoying. It is all what you make of it and looks like you are having a blast!

I am having fun, thank you so much for everything growing up and letting me come here

made me think of you today

Ok. you made me cry again
Love your bud

Love you too ♥

M

ACKNOWLEDGEMENTS

Photography:
Unsplash.com

Ace Maxwell
Adam Wilson
Amit Lahav
Anita Jankovic
Annie Spratt
Calum Lewis
Charles Deloye
Chinh Le Duc
Christian Lue
Claire Mueller
Cullan Smith
Domenico Loia
Domingo Alvarez
Elaine Tu
Emily Bernal
Engin Akyurt
Fatima Akram
Gaelle Marcel
Giorgio Trovato
Inaki Del Olmo
Irene Kredenets
Isaac Azoska
Isabella Fischer
Jas Min
Jeremy Sallee
Joanna Kosinska
Jocelyn Morales
Jonah Brown
Josephine Bredehoft
Juliane Liebermann
Jurien Huggins
Kal Visuals
Kate Trifo
Katherine Hanlon
Kelly Sikkema
Kerri Shaver
Lucrezia Carnelos
Manu Schwendener
Marcel Eberle
Marko Mudrinic
Mufid Majnun
Nathan Dumlao
Nhia Moua
No Revisions
Owen Beard
Pawel Czerwinski
Philippe Jausions
Ruslan Bardash
Scott Webb
Sincerely Media
Slava Taukachou
Taylor Kiser
The Blowup
Towfiqu Barbhuiya
Vera Davidova
Vidar Nordli Mathis
Vitor Monthay
Vyshnavi Bisani
Wesson Wang
Wilhelm Gunkel

Book Design & Illustration by
Stacey Shaller at staceyshallerdesigns.com

Made in the USA
Monee, IL
15 June 2024

59916346R00079